To
FREDA SACHSE
with love

THE ANATOMY OF DRAMA

THE
ANATOMY OF DRAMA

by

MARJORIE BOULTON
M.A., B.Litt.

ROUTLEDGE & KEGAN PAUL

LONDON, BOSTON, MELBOURNE AND HENLEY

First published in 1960
by Routledge & Kegan Paul Limited
39 Store Street,
London. WC1E 7DD,
9 Park Street,
Boston, Mass., 02108, USA,
296 Beaconsfield Parade,
Middle Park, Melbourne,
3206, Australia and
Broadway House, Newtown Road,
Henley-on-Thames,
Oxon. RG9 1EN

Reprinted 1963, 1968, 1971, 1977, 1980 and 1983

Printed in Great Britain by
T. J. Press (Padstow) Ltd
Padstow, Cornwall

© Marjorie Boulton 1960

ISBN 0 7100 1101 6 (c)
ISBN 0 7100 6090 4 (p)

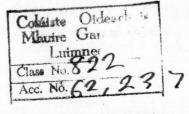

FOREWORD

THIS small book is not intended as an original contribution to literary criticism; it is no more than a popularization; but I hope it may also be no less. Its aim is: to help the person with no access, or rare access, to the professional theatre, towards a clearer notion of the function and nature of drama and a greater enjoyment of plays. It is intended especially for older schoolchildren, students and others who, for examination purposes, are obliged, not to see plays for pleasure, but to study the text of plays in detail. This, as well as his genius, accounts for the high proportion of attention given to Shakespeare. I have tried, in fact, to write the book on drama that I wish I had read when I was about fourteen.

Relatively few people in England today can see stage plays at all frequently. Such is our splendid library service, however, that hardly any literate person is unable to read as many plays as anyone may reasonably wish. This book is mostly for the reader of plays; it may, I hope, make the reading of plays a more satisfying experience—and the study of set plays for examinations rather more meaningful.

I am most grateful to the following for their kind permission to use copyright material:

Christopher Fry and Oxford University Press, for two passages from *The Lady's Not For Burning*.

Messrs. Chatto and Windus for two passages from A. A. Milne's *To Have the Honour*.

Terence Rattigan and A. D. Peters for the passage from *The Browning Version*.

Foreword

J. I. M. Stewart and Messrs. Longmans Green and Co., for the passage from *Character and Motive in Shakespeare*.

I am also grateful to numerous schoolchildren and students who, by their interpretations of drama, have taught me more than they imagined I was teaching them. I hope that in return this book may add something to the fun of close study.

MARJORIE BOULTON

Stoke-on-Trent
May 1959

CONTENTS

Part One

CONVENTIONS

I. LITERATURE THAT WALKS

Snug: You can never bring in a wall. What say you, Bottom?
Bottom: Some man or other must present Wall; and let him have some
           plaster, or some loam, or some rough-cast about him, to
           signify wall; and let him hold his fingers thus, and through
           that cranny shall Pyramus and Thisby whisper.
                        A Midsummer Night's Dream, Act III, Sc. 1.

THERE is an enormous difference between a play and any other form of literature. A play is not really a piece of literature for reading. A true play is three-dimensional; it is literature that walks and talks before our eyes. It is not intended that the eye shall perceive marks on paper and the imagination turn them into sights, sounds and actions; the text of the play is meant to be translated into sights, sounds and actions which occur literally and physically on a stage. Though in fact plays are often read in silence, if we are to study drama at all intelligently we must always keep this in mind.

Some visual imagination was needed by the spectator of a Shakespeare play in the Shakespearian theatre:

> And so our scene must to the battle fly;
> Where—O for pity,—we shall much disgrace,
> With four or five most vile and ragged foils,
> Right ill dispos'd in brawl ridiculous,
> The name of Agincourt. Yet sit and see;
> Minding true things by what their mockeries be.
>   *Henry V*, Prologue to Act V

Beautiful language was used to suggest sunrise, nightfall or noon where nowadays lighting effects would be used:

> Light thickens, and the crow

3

Makes wing to the rooky wood;
Good things of day begin to droop and drowse,
Whiles night's black agents to their preys do rouse.

Macbeth, Act III, Sc. 2

The modern dramatist usually gives instructions for detailed scenery and the kind of visual imagination demanded by the early theatre is nowadays demanded chiefly by the radio drama, in which the words, perhaps with a few sound effects, again have to do all the work.

However, no play makes the same demands on our visual imagination as any novel, descriptive or narrative poem, or short story. The actions and conversations take place before our very eyes; or, if there are actions in the play so violent or distressing that they cannot be represented on the stage, they can be described by characters who are present on the stage and show all the appropriate signs of horror and revulsion. Even this is more violent in emotional impact than the experience of merely reading a description in the third person.

To see a play is, for most people, a more exciting and memorable experience than to read a novel.

The concentration and intensity of emotion is caused by our actually seeing and hearing the events represented; but the special character of drama also lays considerable limitations upon it. In a way it is the form of literary art most restricted by conventions. The conventions are of two kinds: those that make for the intensity and concentration of drama, the violent impact; and those that protect the audience from too violent an experience or that are enforced by mere physical possibility. The former are by far the more interesting from the point of view of literary criticism, but the student of drama needs the knowledge of both in order to appreciate dramatic technique to the full.

While anything that can be represented on the stage can be conveyed to an audience with much greater intensity than by any other literary means, not everything that is material

4

for literature can be material for drama, for not everything can be represented on the stage. Physical possibility plays a part in this. The first and most important of these physical limitations is that the drama must deal with human affairs exclusively, because it is to be performed by human beings. This may not sound like a major restriction; but when we think of the part played by landscape in the novels of Thomas Hardy, the non-human personalities of H. G. Wells's scientific romances, the animal characters in Virginia Woolf's *Flush*, Colette's *La Chatte* or Henry Williamson's *Tarka the Otter*, or the sea in the novels of Conrad, we realize that it is a very real limitation on the subject matter. It is possible to represent a landscape by means of painted cloth, and stage landscapes are often so beautiful as to add considerably to the emotional effect of the play; but it is not possible to give a landscape life and personality by this means. The sea can be represented; even moving waves can be shown by mechanical devices; and sometimes real water has been used in a theatre; but a dramatization of Conrad's *Typhoon* would be beyond the resources of even the most lavishly equipped modern theatre. Comic animals can appear in pantomime and serious animals in such allegorical plays as Maeterlinck's *The Blue Bird* or Čapek's *The Insect Play*; but a real cat or dog among human beings cannot well have an important part. Live animals have been used on the stage; there was even a play produced in 1814, *The Dog of Montargis*, in which a dog was the chief character; horses, doves and sparrows have appeared in the theatre; but these freaks of production have usually been spectacular rather than truly dramatic. In Alex Comfort's fine novel *The Power House* and in H. G. Wells's short story *The Lord of the Dynamos*, a moving machine is so important as to have personality; this, too, is almost impossible in drama, though it might be practicable in experimental radio drama.

Moreover, very little can be shown on the stage that cannot be represented by physically normal adults. Nothing much further from the physically normal than the hump of

Conventions

Richard III or the blindness and lameness of Sydney in Somerset Maugham's *For Services Rendered* is possible on the stage. The giants and dwarfs of romance have no place on the legitimate stage, simply because real giants and dwarfs do not train as actors, since their opportunities would be very limited. Extreme deformities or injuries and revolting disease cannot be shown on the stage as they would shock the spectators too much, although they could usually be simulated quite well by make-up.

There are many fine novels on the theme of childhood, but talented child actors are rare and the employment of children on the stage is rightly subject to stringent control. The technique of good acting takes so long to learn that it is almost impossible to have, say, Juliet adequately represented by an actress of fourteen, which is Juliet's age according to Shakespeare. Unfortunately, too, the public is so fond of children on stage and screen that, as with musical prodigies, a child actor arouses a kind of enthusiasm that has little to do with dramatic art.

The good actor has to have a sound constitution and quite considerable powers of endurance, for the life is strenuous; but the drama is restricted by the physical capacities of normally healthy people.

The possibilities of drama are also limited by the intractability of material objects. H. G. Wells's *The Invisible Man* has been filmed, using trick photography; but it could never be successfully dramatized on the stage as we know it. The miracles that can be represented on the stage, the physical catastrophes that can occur, are few. It is also necessary to remember that not everything that can somehow be represented on the stage can be made convincing. Noel Coward's *Blithe Spirit* has a ghost as a principal character; this can be given an illusion of reality by the skilled use of make-up and lighting effects; people can appear or disappear by means of trapdoors specially designed for stage use; brief flight is possible by the use of wires; but the playwright has to remember that there comes a point in such

6

mechanical tricks when the audience is so interested in 'how it is done' that all dramatic illusion disappears. More spectacular special effects are used in pantomime and similar entertainments than in true drama, because then the audience wishes to marvel rather than to be convinced.

Ordinary human events, however, may be difficult to show on the stage. Travel, a common theme on the films, cannot easily be represented on the stage. A battle, an air-raid or even a football match cannot be represented at all realistically on the stage except by the comments of a spectator or some other conventional device; lighting effects can suggest a fire, as in Christopher Fry's *Venus Observed*, but Shaw's Saint Joan must be burned at the stake off the stage; and it is difficult to represent the more drastic effects of wind, rain, snow or a volcanic eruption, though it is easy to produce the sound of wind or rain, to blow someone's hat off or show someone as wet.

Numerous changes of scene are not convenient on the stage, however simple and usual the scenes may be. The very frequent changes of scene in Shakespeare, often with scenes as short as this:

> *Scene 2. The Same. The Field of Battle.*
> *Alarum. Enter Brutus and Messala.*
>
> *Brutus:* Ride, ride, Messala, ride and give these bills
> Unto the legions on the other side. (*Loud Alarum*)
> Let them set on at once, for I perceive
> But cold demeanour in Octavius' wing,
> And sudden push gives them the overthrow.
> Ride, ride, Messala; let them all come down.
>   (*Exeunt*)
>
>   *Julius Caesar*, Act V

were possible only because the Elizabethans did not have scenery as we know it. When modern scenery is used the scene cannot be changed without lowering the curtain, interrupting the action of the play and breaking the illusion by the clatter and bustle of scene-shifters. (There are various mechanical devices, such as the use of a revolving platform, hydraulic lifts and elaborate systems of hanging scenery that make scene-shifting easier; but these, too, have their limitations and are very costly.) This physical difficulty is one reason for the great popularity in modern times of the play in which, though there are three acts, only one scene is used. Examples of this are J. B. Priestley's *Dangerous Corner*, A. A. Milne's *To Have the Honour* and Bernard Shaw's *Candida*. More than two changes of scene present considerable difficulties, though there are still plays as episodic as Auden and Isherwood's *The Dog Beneath the Skin* with fifteen different scenes or, in the less experimental vein, James Bridie's *A Sleeping Clergyman* with nine different scenes.

Plays have been set in some curious places: in a dug-out (*Journey's End*), on the side of a mountain (part of *The Ascent of F6*), in a dentist's surgery (part of *You Never Can Tell*), on a steamer (*Anna Christie*), in a railway carriage and on a station (*The Little Man*) and even inside a burial vault (*A Phoenix Too Frequent*). In general, however, the ordinary room in a private house, perhaps with period furnishings but having doors and windows, is still the favourite setting for a play. This is not only because, after all, human life, even at its most dramatic, still goes on mostly in ordinary rooms, but also because unusual settings are more difficult and expensive to prepare. Because of this difficulty in changing the scene frequently the playwright may resort to such contrivances as: to bring characters together with coincidences more numerous than are usual in real life; to allow various things to happen in unlikely places or at least not in the most likely place; to tell the audience various things by letting someone on the stage relate them, instead of showing them; to make use of letters for the same purpose; to allow people to overhear the kind of conversation no sane person allows to be overheard in real life; to pretend that the auditorium is a scene being looked at or to place someone at a window or other look-out to describe what it is not convenient to show.

Literature that Walks

These are the main physical limitations on the possibilities of drama. The actual length of a play is also restricted by such considerations, not only for the actors but for the audience, since even sitting still is tiring if it goes on for too long.

The other restrictions imposed by considerations not purely artistic are those of seemliness; the shock of an experience more intense than reading must not be so intense as to do harm. The stage censorship in Great Britain, and still more in some less democratic or more puritanical countries, is often stupid; but good taste and psychological prudence impose a kind of censorship even when the law does not interfere. In a novel it is quite possible and usual to describe, in sufficient detail to give a sense of reality, such things as murder, torture, severe injuries, deformities and disfigurements, unpleasant illnesses, death, however horrible, and also such things as sexual relationships of various kinds. In a novel it is permissible to speak of anything so long as we avoid a few very gross expressions and occasionally use a circumlocution. Words printed on paper do not easily shock us deeply. Many very mild and humane people love to read detective fiction, 'Westerns' or war novels; and if we were not able to read of violence and other disturbing subjects with reasonable calm the ordinary daily paper would endanger our sanity. What we are actually prepared to look at is more limited; our imaginations do not present these disturbing ideas to us as vividly as an actual three-dimensional representation. It is quite inoffensive to say in a novel, 'Doreen took off her clothes slowly, wandered round the room once or twice before she found the pyjamas she had thrown carelessly on to the floor, then put them on and climbed into bed.' Now, there is nothing upsetting in a naked body for a healthy-minded sensible person; but to show this on the stage would be felt, not only by prudes but by most normal people, as an unseemly and embarrassing display. We should feel that it was not fair to ask the actress personating Doreen to go through a display that might be humiliating for her, even if the British censorship did not for-

9

bid such a scene. This natural feeling of reticence applies with still more force to anything which is intrinsically ugly or evil.

The actual legal censorship in Britain is somewhat capricious in operation and comes under discussion fairly often. It has tended to support our ostrich-like timidity in discussing some serious problems, while frequently allowing plays and films which glorify violence or money-making, inculcate attitudes of childish irresponsibility, vulgarize noble themes or treat genuine misfortunes as comic. The difficulty of censorship is that there are a good many plays which are works of great artistic merit, or treat an important subject of sociology, morals or religion seriously, or both, but which might be too violently disturbing for very young people or people who are not mentally stable. Examples of plays that have suffered at the hands of the censorship in this country are Shelley's *The Cenci*, a play on a terrible theme from history, but in no way offensive to good taste; Shaw's *Mrs. Warren's Profession*, a strongly moral and indeed characteristically puritanical drama on an unpleasant social theme; Granville-Barker's *Waste*, a dignified treatment of a genuine problem; Laurence Housman's *Victoria Regina*, not on grounds of impropriety but because it dealt with royal personages; and Lilian Hellman's *The Children's Hour*, a very powerful and disturbing tragedy which certainly ought to be for adults only, but for many adults would be a moving experience and not objectionable. Perhaps the best solution to this problem would be something equivalent to the X certificate in the film industry—a classification which completely protects very young people from sights which might be too disturbing for them or lead, by misunderstanding, to vice or crime, but allows adults to see serious and thought-provoking films treating of themes adults ought to know about and consider sympathetically. There is, of course, no guarantee that every person over sixteen is balanced and intelligent enough to be exposed to disturbing matter; but at some point in life, at least in a democracy, people must be assumed to be competent to look after themselves. One of the unfortunate side-effects of the censorship is that if something is banned people with dirty minds immediately develop an intense and unwholesome curiosity about it, and if it is later released some of the people who rush to see it may be the very people who ought not to be seeing it because they are already not in a good state of mental health.[1]

Another limitation is imposed on the dramatist by the limited intelligence of the average audience. This is not a joke, nor is it cynicism; anyone who has ever tried to explain something to another person knows that the human capacity for absorbing something at a first hearing, or absorbing it accurately, is small. Now, if I do not understand a poem at a first reading—and if it is a great poem I probably do not understand it fully—I can read it again as often as I like; I can take it to someone who appreciates that type of poetry better than I do and ask for help; I can take down my dictionary and look up a word, or I can look up allusions in reference books. The same is true of a novel. If, in a novel, I become confused about the relationships of the characters, nothing prevents my turning back to sort them out; if the ideas or problems are unfamiliar I may pause whenever I please to think about them. When I go to the theatre the situation is very different, for if I do not grasp immediately what is going on I have lost it for good and only a second visit to the play, or a reading of it, will clear up my bewilderment. Some subtleties that would be admirable in fiction are useless in the theatre, because the audience cannot react quickly enough to grasp them while following the dialogue and general development.

In a play there are often repetitions even of quite simple

---

[1] Two amusing examples of the frequent inanity of censorship are: Jawaharlal Nehru, perhaps one of the most ethically-minded statesmen alive, intervened to allow Olivier's film of *Hamlet* to circulate uncut in India when the prudes objected to the 'foul language'; and a few years ago in England a serious and responsible play on a social problem won a licence only on the intervention of a royal personage.

facts, careful explanations, addressing of people by their names more frequently than in real conversation and various over-simplifications which to the reader of a play in a study may seem almost infantile. These are, however, devices for ensuring that the audience grasps whatever it is necessary for it to know for the enjoyment of the play. Similarly, the play-wright must not ask his audience to take in too much at once. Shaw has often been blamed for interpolating passages of slapstick farce into his argumentative and provocative plays. Certainly his slapstick is sometimes crude as compared with the rest of his work; but the average audience cannot listen to uninterrupted argument for two hours; and *Getting Married*, which is an orgy of brilliant talk with hardly any action, is certainly not Shaw's best play.

The matters which have so far been discussed are relatively minor matters as compared with the use of conventions to achieve concentration, which is perhaps the central requirement of dramatic technique. Conventions of decency, the physical capacities of human beings and the possibilities of stage technique may change; the possibilities of a well-equipped modern theatre for realistic and complicated effects are already remarkable; but the artistic needs have remained more or less constant throughout literary history. Tragedy must offer an accumulation of strong emotions; comedy must offer some kind of continuous and preferably cumulative amusement; a play which does not excite us sufficiently in the manner appropriate to the type of play is an unsatisfying play; and this intense excitement is achieved by concentration.

So far as I know the first attempt at making a formula for achieving dramatic concentration was Aristotle (384–322 B.C.) who in his famous *Poetics* (of which several English translations are available) made the suggestions that eventually gave rise to the theory of the Three Unities. Aristotle wrote of the need for what other critics have called the Unity of Action; the plot of a play must be, as it were, all in one piece. Out of this developed the later and stricter theories of the classicists, of whom Racine in France was typical: the Unity of Place prescribes that the whole play must have only one scene, because it is absurd to imagine that we are first in Rome and then, in a few minutes, in Alexandria; the Unity of Time is usually taken to mean that the events of a play must not extend over more than twenty-four hours, though some strict classicists reduced even this limit and tried to make the action quite continuous, with the time taken by the events of the play and the time taken to show them identical. Dr. Johnson pointed out, very sensibly, that we do not believe ourselves in Rome or Alexandria anyway, and if we can imagine ourselves in one place where we are not we can quite well imagine ourselves in another; but often a play set in one place may seem more realistic than one in which the scene is frequently changed. Plays frequently extend over very long periods of imaginary time; *Antony and Cleopatra*, *Saint Joan*, William Douglas Home's *The Thistle and the Rose* and Gordon Daviot's *Richard of Bordeaux* extend over months or even years; and Shaw's *Back to Methusaleh* begins in the Garden of Eden and ends 'as far as thought can reach'! Excluding geniuses such as Shakespeare and Shaw, who are a law unto themselves, the most satisfying plays do often seem to be those in which the action is spread over only a short period of time. Perhaps this is because in real life we seldom have prolonged periods of tension, of long sequences of dramatic events without some periods of relief or interruptions by the mere humdrum routine of life. We may find it difficult, too, to follow a play in which, as in Bridie's *A Sleeping Clergyman* or Arnold Bennett's *Milestones*, several generations follow one another and the manners and customs of several periods are shown in succession. However, these plays and others of their type have often been successful, so no fixed rule can be made.

The Unities of Place and Time, then, are no more than formal conventions, dictated in part by the real needs of the theatre, but capable of being frequently broken without disaster. They may contribute to the concentration of emotion;

13

but they are not necessary to it. *Othello* is perhaps one of the most concentrated plays ever written—certainly one of the most concentrated of English plays—in the emotional experience provided, the accumulation of pity and terror and the dreadful, inexorable speed with which the play moves to its tragic close; but there are many drastic changes of scene in the play, and the handling of time is, from the strictly literal or mathematical point of view, so odd and awkward that much criticism has been written about the 'double time-scheme in *Othello*'. A play that keeps strictly to all the unities but has no true dramatic quality, that has no lifelike characters, no vigorous dialogue, no gripping action, may be a miserable failure. The Unity of Action, however, is more than a convention. It is almost always necessary if the play is to hold an audience continuously.

In a novel it is possible to have a great many incidental episodes and sub-plots, even, sometimes, whole separate stories incorporated into the book; an example of the last device is the beautiful allegory of the development of the soul in Olive Schreiner s *Story of an African Farm*, an allegory which can stand by itself, although the whole novel tells the story of the development of two souls in a more literal, naturalistic way. It is possible to introduce a character, not to play an important part in the unfolding of the plot, but simply for the sake of comic or pathetic effect. A novel may also have, as in the work of Charles Reade or Dickens, passages of social or moral criticism or even literary criticism interpolated by the author, who openly speaks in his own person. In a play this is impossible. The action all takes place in a short time of actual performance, and there is no room for ornaments and episodes. Literature that walks must not carry heavy loads as well.

It is difficult to find a plot that gives this unity; it usually means making things rather simpler and considerably swifter than they are in real life;[1] but the concentration that can

---

[1] Some selection is, of course, made in all art. If we describe a single day in a human life in its full detail the result is something as huge as

14

thus be achieved is very satisfying. An example of this will be found in the Greek tragedy *Antigone*, by Sophocles—a play, incidentally, that obeys all the classical Unities, for it takes place in one locality and the action is uninterrupted except by the Chorus, which recites didactic or reflective poetry to punctuate the action. Even when the play is performed merely by students still holding books, as I have several times seen it done, it remains powerful because of this terrific compression of the emotion into a small space.

At the beginning of the play a conflict of duties is represented. The two sons of Oedipus the late King of Thebes are dead after fighting each other; the two daughters, Antigone and Ismene, survive and Thebes is ruled by Creon. It is Antigone's duty to bury her brother who was in the wrong, for his credit in this world and his welfare in the next; but the king has given orders that the traitor shall lie unburied. Family piety is an unbreakable obligation; but legally constituted authority must be obeyed, for the stability and safety of every community depends upon this. The king is not a mere tyrant; his intentions are good and the brother was really in the wrong. This dilemma, strengthened by Creon's decree that anyone who buries the corpse shall be put to death, is a genuine one and very painful. Ismene chooses to obey authority, partly from real belief in it, partly from fear; Antigone, the stronger character, buries her brother in defiance of orders, is arrested and is at once condemned to death; she shows a heroic fortitude and defiance made more touching by her natural regrets for the denial of marriage and motherhood which her sacrifice involves. Just at this point, when our emotions are already much stirred, a fresh dilemma arises.

The king's son, Haemon, is betrothed to Antigone. He asks for her to be pardoned; Creon refuses. Thus there is a double conflict between 'love' and 'duty'; Haemon wishes to be loyal to his father but also to save the life of his beloved,

James Joyce's *Ulysses*, and while this is a great book no one wants a shelf full of similar books. But the selection in drama is much more rigorous.

and his conflict is made more painful by his sense that Creon's decision is morally and politically unsound; Creon would like to indulge his son, but feels that any weakness at this moment would endanger the safety of the State; his conflict is made more violent by his resentment of the criticisms made by Haemon and the Chorus. Again these are real dilemmas and there is no happy solution. The resolution of the conflicts is in death: Antigone dies by her own hand in the cave where she has been immured to starve, just before Creon, afraid of the wrath of the gods, has sent someone to liberate her; Haemon kills himself; the Queen kills herself, distracted with grief for the loss of her son; and Creon is left alone, a broken, humbled man scarcely able to speak coherently. The whole play thus moves with dreadful rapidity to its close; we are never able to relax; and the close appears to be the only possible one. The Greek convention of the period that only two of the principal characters should be talking on the stage at once heightens our awareness of the clash of personalities and principles. There is no trace of any subplot or decorative episode. The words, even in translation, have a telling force and dignity that makes it almost impossible to ruin the play so long as they are spoken clearly and with dignity. A novel can do much more than this; but this it cannot do.

The reader may like to examine *Othello*, *Macbeth* or *Lear*, or a good modern tragedy such as Tennessee Williams's *A Streetcar Named Desire*, Terence Rattigan's *The Deep Blue Sea*, Christa Winsloe's *Children in Uniform*, or Somerset Maugham's *The Sacred Flame* to see how in each case concentration is achieved through the essential unity of the action and the speed with which it moves.

The unity of action is equally important to give concentration in comedy, though here, of course, the concentration is not of violent emotions but of amusement. Comic concentration is the close packing of amusing episodes and witty remarks. Most of us who are not boiled codfish make an amusing remark sometimes; we may rarely be privileged

Literature that Walks

even to make an amusing remark so neat that everyone within hearing laughs, but no one in normal conversation produces as many epigrams, jokes or beautifully timed repartees as the characters, not portrayed as otherwise extraordinary or gifted people, in the plays of Shaw, Congreve, Oscar Wilde, Vanbrugh or even A. A. Milne, the last coming perhaps nearest to ordinary conversation.

Mirabell: I have seen him, he promises to be an extraordinary person; I think you have the honour to be related to him.

Fainall: Yes; he is half-brother to this Witwoud by a former wife, who was sister to my Lady Wishfort, my wife's mother. If you marry Millamant, you must call cousins too.

Mirabell: I had rather be his relation than his acquaintance.

Fainall: He comes to town to equip himself for travel.

Mirabell: For Travel! Why, the man that I mean is above forty.

Fainall: No matter for that; 'tis for the honour of England, that all Europe should know we have blockheads of all ages.

Mirabell: I wonder there is not an act of parliament to save the credit of the nation, and prohibit the export of fools.

Fainall: By no means, 'tis better as it is; 'tis better to trade with a little loss, than to be quite eaten up, with being overstocked.

Mirabell: Pray, are the follies of this knight-errant, and those of the squire, his brother, anything related?

Fainall: Not at all, Witwoud grows by the knight, like a medlar grafted on a crab. One will melt in your mouth, and t'other set your teeth upon edge; one is all pulp, and the other all core.

Mirabell: So one will be rotten before he be ripe, and the other will be rotten without ever being ripe at all.

CONGREVE: *The Way of the World*

Conventions

Most people would agree that in real life the person who sets out consciously to be a wit is a poor companion and often unsympathetic. In watching a comedy we are delighted with this kind of conversation.

Similarly, in real life comic episodes do frequently occur. They may be of the kind found in farce, as when my mother found herself half-way upstairs with a milk bottle and re-traced her steps to find that she had indeed left the alarm clock outside the front door; or they may be of the kind found in high comedy, as in the episode I can vouch for of a man taking out to dinner two women to whom he was pay-ing court simultaneously, in the expectation that they would be embarrassed and shamed, and being disconcerted when, having a good deal of sympathy for one another, they carried on an animated conversation, obviously about him, in a language he could not understand. But such episodes do not normally pile up, in life, with the speed of good comedy; if they did, life would be altogether too strenuous for us, and we should not look back on these incidents with so much amusement.

Gammer Gurton's Needle is one of the earliest and crudest of English comedies; but even in this there is a remarkable rapid accumulation of comic episodes, with a climax admir-able in its way, though savouring more of custard pie than of Congreve. Shakespeare's *Comedy of Errors* is a good ex-ample of the comedy of odd episodes without much charac-ter interest; mistakes of identity crowd upon one another un-til all the characters are giddy. Character is more important in *Twelfth Night*, which is beautiful as well as funny, but again the comic remarks and comic situations follow one an-other much faster than in real life. In Oscar Wilde's comedies everyone talks like Oscar Wilde, and it has been said with considerably less truth that in Bernard Shaw's comedies everyone talks like Bernard Shaw; certainly everyone in a play talks much better at all times than most of us do at any time. This is not falsity, not bad art, there is a difference be-tween heightening and distortion.

18

Literature that Walks

This is, I trust, enough to make it clear that the special nature of drama, its literal, three-dimensional visibility and audibility, its violent impact, give it certain inevitable limitations based on human and physical capabilities, that the drama is thus governed more strictly by a set of conventions than are other forms of art; but that, on the other hand, the very restrictions of the dramatic conventions contribute to the impact of drama upon an audience by concentrating the emotion or amusement. There is, however, a necessary condition for this which will be discussed in the next chapter.

II. SO WE MUST MAKE IT WALK

Reader, it is impossible we should know what sort of a person thou
wilt be; for, perhaps, thou mayest be as learned in human nature as
Shakespeare himself was, and, perhaps thou mayest be no wiser than
some of his editors.

HENRY FIELDING: *Tom Jones*

THE artistic conventions of drama arise out of the fact
that drama is performed, yet the student who is
working on a 'set play' for an examination, or studying the history of the drama, frequently studies the play entirely as something to be read. Perhaps it is read in a classroom smelling of ink and chalk, perhaps in a study-bedroom
which is small, chilly and unimpressive; the student makes
pencilled annotations in the margin and prepares answers to
expected questions. This is not useless, but such study of
drama misses the point; if a play is meant to be read (primarily, for there is nothing to stop us reading a good play!)
there is no need for it to be suitable for performance and it
need not be a real play. Indeed, a play is often altered in production, when, at a rehearsal, the playwright himself, or the
producer, is able to see some practical difficulty or devise
some improvement that had not occurred to him before.

A printed play is only the recipe for a performance; the
play must be 'cooked'—that is produced—before it gives the
kind of satisfaction it was intended to give. This is one
reason why the study of a 'set play' in school or college can
be maddeningly tedious, even more so than the study of a
set novel.

Here is a fragment from Marlowe's *Dr. Faustus*, in
print:

Faustus:	Why, have you any pain that torture others?
Mephistophilis:	A great as have the human souls of men.
	But tell me, Faustus, shall I have thy soul?
	And I will be thy slave and wait on thee,
	And give thee more than thou hast wit to ask.
Faustus:	Aye, Mephistophilis, I'll give it him.
Mephistophilis:	Then, Faustus, stab thine arm courageously,
	And bind thy soul, that at some certain day
	Great Lucifer may claim it for his own;
	And then be thou as great as Lucifer.
Faustus:	(*stabbing his arm*)
	Lo, Mephistophilis, for love of thee,
	Faustus hath cut his arm, and with his blood
	Assures himself to be great Lucifer's,
	Chief lord and regent of perpetual night.
	View here this blood that trickles from my arm,
	(*Catches the blood in a cup.*)
	And let it be propitious to thy wish.
Mephistophilis:	But, Faustus,
	Write it in manner of a deed of gift.
Faustus:	Ah, so I do! but, Mephistophilis,
	My blood congeals, and I can write no more.
Mephistophilis:	I'll fetch thee fire to dissolve it straight.
	(*Exit*)
Faustus:	What might this staying of my blood portend?
	Is it unwilling I should write this bill?
	Why streams it not, that I may write afresh?
	Faustus gives to thee his soul: O there it stayed!
	Why shouldst thou not? is not this soul thine own?
	Then write again, *Faustus gives to thee his soul.*

Conventions

(*Enter Mephistophilis with the chafer of fire.*)

Mephistophilis: See, Faustus, here is fire; set it on.

Faustus: So now the blood begins to clear again; Now will I make an end immediately.

Mephistophilis: What will I not do, to obtain his soul? (*Aside*)

Faustus: *Consummatum est*, this bill is ended, And Faustus hath bequeathed his soul to Lucifer.

Now our appreciation of this scene when we read it depends, as does all appreciation of a play in print, on two things, our previous experience of the living theatre and the vividness of our visual imagination. If we are sufficiently accustomed to the theatre to be able to picture the play on the stage, it helps a great deal; and without imagination there is no mental activity of any depth, let alone the especially demanding and sympathetic activity involved in enjoying art. But unless we have more experience of production and theatregoing than the average student living in the provinces can have, our power to visualize a play as acted from reading the printed version is very inadequate. Imagination is, moreover, a faculty many of us have neglected to train; it can be trained, either with the help of a teacher or in solitude, and indeed it might well be argued that the practice of reading plays in silence is quite good as a training for the imagination; but there must also be some experience of produced plays to begin the process.

A sensitive, intelligent reader in a study will certainly find a few thrills in this extract. The theme of a man selling his soul to the devil is powerful enough to compel interest. There is the grim irony of 'My blood congeals'—to Faustus just an annoying failure of the ink, but reminding us of the feeling often called 'my blood congealing' or 'my blood running cold' which is associated with the presence of the horrible or the supernatural. There is the still more dreadful irony

22

of Faustus' use of the phrase *Consummatum est* ('It is finished') as the seal of his damnation when it is so familiar in a context of redemption. There is the sinister fearfulness of the 'unwilling' blood. But the stage directions give quite a wrong impression when read in print.

In print they appear to be an interruption of the dialogue. In fact, they are nearly always indications of what the actor is to do while speaking. An actor who said, 'View here this blood that trickles from my arm', then stopped speaking and pretended to collect some blood from his imaginary wound, then resumed speaking, having put the cup down, and said, 'And let it be propitious for thy wish', would seem intolerably deliberate and even rather absurd. He would also draw too much concentrated attention to actions in which he was pretending to do something no actor could reasonably be expected to do in reality night after night. All the words, both speeches and stage directions, are no more than the recipe for the performance to be arranged by a producer.

On the stage, with competent acting, this scene springs to life and is terrifying. I have vivid memories of an excellent simple production by a small travelling company; they had no special effects or costly scenery such as would have been beyond their means; they simply carried out Marlowe's recipe in a workman-like manner. However, thus we saw, instead of having to imagine, or perhaps failing to imagine, a quietly dressed, bearded scholar talking with a Mephistophilis whose make-up and voice rendered him continuously sinister without melodrama; we heard the despair in his voice when he said, 'As great as have the human souls of men'; we saw Faustus draw a dagger from his belt and pretend to open a vein in his arm, wincing slightly as the skin was pierced; we fancied that we could see the resistance of the skin to the sharp point; we saw Faustus press a cup to the imaginary but now real-seeming wound and take up parchment and quill to write the deed of gift, in a kind of dreadful casualness, not understanding the finality of his bond; we saw him brood on clotting blood that we could easily believe was clogging the point of his pen; and when Mephistophilis appeared carrying a silver basin in which green flames were leaping, we shivered, for it seemed a bowl of fire dredged up from the infernal lake. There sat Faustus at his desk, not noticing the strangeness of the fire, complacently warming his cup of blood and finishing his contract with his academic blasphemy. Now, as I read the scene again, I can visualize all this; but all this detail had been worked out, together with the costumes and the lighting of the stage, by producer and actors, doubtless after discussion, trial and error; no one could picture the scene in its full terror at a first reading.

Dr. Johnson, the greatest of British eighteenth-century critics, said many wise things about Shakespeare, but one of the least wise things he ever said in his life was surely, 'A play read affects the mind like a play acted'.[1] Perhaps he himself had a freakishly vivid imagination, or, on the other hand, perhaps he was singularly insensible to the experience of the theatre; but for the vast majority of people this is simply not true. We have only to think of the number of people who cannot read Shakespeare except as a duty, but to whom a Shakespeare play performed at the theatre is a treat. Moreover, there are many modern plays, such as those of Noel Coward, which seem very unimpressive when read as mere scripts, but can reduce an audience to helpless mirth, or, sometimes, move them greatly, when performed at the right speed and with the right actions. This is not a weakness in Mr. Coward; it means that he is very much a writer for the living theatre. A good theatre manager or producer ought to be able to see whether a script will thus come to vivid life in production; but the general public cannot usually be expected to do this. The contention which dictates the whole method of this book is that a play read does *not* affect the mind like a play acted and that therefore the study of a play should always be closely related to the possibility of staging it.

This may be a convenient place to remind the reader that

[1] *Preface to Shakespeare*, 1765.

So We Must Make It Walk

drama now has a number of subsidiary forms other than the
stage play. The *opera* combines drama with music and generally with a good deal of spectacle; but it is a standing joke
that in opera the music is so much more important than the
words that the words (*libretto*) may be fatuous or even in-
audible. *Radio* provides a type of drama very different from
the stage play; scenery is non-existent and actions can be
implied only by comments or sound effects; and the audience may consist in one sense of one person in one room,
though usually the total audience for a radio play is very
large. But an audience scattered over the whole country cannot have the collective experience the theatre provides. The
laws of drama as regards concentration, plot, characterization and so on, all apply with equal force to radio drama.
The scripts of radio dramas are even more difficult to
appreciate by silent reading than the scripts of stage plays.
Television brings us back to visible drama and often, at
present, to the assembled audience, since invitations to
go to another house to see the television are not uncommon; the art of specifically television drama has perhaps
not yet reached maturity, but television also enables normal
theatre plays to be produced, in a modified form, for audiences out of reach of theatres, and should thus help to improve the appreciation of drama in the country. *Film*, now
a great and adult art at its best, weds drama to the art of
photography in a new form that deserves to be taken seriously and has enormous advantages in that it can do away
with many of the physical limitations of the theatre, shifting
the scene continually and showing many things impossible
on the stage, by means of trick photography; it can also
bring great drama and first-class professional acting to communities that can support no live theatre; and from the point
of view of the public it has also the advantage of being cheap;
the cinema, too, is often more comfortable than the theatre.
Unfortunately, the film industry is also the most vulgarized
and commercialized of the forms of drama; the film-going
public has not yet learned to boycott childish films and de-

25

mand a high standard of art. (The average theatre audience is at least a good deal more discriminating than the average film audience, and, at least in my experience, is often more attentive.) In the film industry the 'star' cult, with irrelevant newspaper gossip about the personal lives of film actors and actresses, excessive and vulgar publicity and a disproportionate stress on physical attractiveness rather than acting ability increases the vulgarization of an art which can be noble.

The *puppet theatre*, with glove puppets, rod puppets or puppets operated by strings (*marionettes*) has a special technique of its own and sometimes reaches high artistic levels, though obviously its limitations are greater than those of the live theatre. This form of drama is more important in Czechoslovakia, Germany and parts of the Far East than in England, though 'Punch and Judy' is still popular in English holiday resorts; however, puppetry is gaining ground as a very valuable educational activity that combines craftwork with English work and both with very wholesome training in co-operation. There are also the *variety show*, the modern *pantomime* and the true *mime*, all of which are offshoots of the drama, though they do not come within the scope of this book; the form of drama most often found in the lively home or other small community is the *charade*, from which people who have little to do with drama can learn a good deal about its basic requirements and problems; and much of the play of children has dramatic aspects. I have not the requisite knowledge to treat at length of anything but the legitimate drama of the live theatre, nor in this book room to treat of other branches of the art; but much of what applies to the stage play applies to the other branches.

Some people make a distinction between 'stage drama' and 'closet drama'. A closet drama, in this context, is not one that would be better put away in a cupboard and forgotten, but a play which is better read than acted. Perhaps there really are such things; perhaps this is true of Shelley's *Prometheus Unbound* and *The Cenci*, Byron's *Manfred* and

So We Must Make It Walk

Cain,[1] Wordsworth's *The Borderers* and Addison's *Cato*,[2] possibly even Stephen Spender's *Trial of a Judge* and Anne Ridler's *The Mask*—not her other plays, which are very actable; but in general a play that is better not produced is not a true play. If, like all those mentioned above, it has some literary merit, and may be, like the Shelley plays, a work of genius, it is not so much a play as a poem, narrative or argument written in dialogue form. John Steinbeck, in America, has written a new kind of 'closet drama' in what he calls his 'play-novelettes', short novels that could be played simply by lifting out the dialogue. Steinbeck's 'play-novelettes' include *The Moon is Down*, *Of Mice and Men* and *Burning Bright*. The first two have been produced as plays and films with success. *Burning Bright*, though a noble and touching novel on a profound and unusual theme, is much less realistic in its dialogue and I do not think it would seem convincing on the stage; perhaps this is true closet-drama.

The plays of great dramatists—and it is possible to be a very great writer without being a great dramatist—are always better acted than read. In future I shall refer to the written play, the sheets of paper filled with dialogue and stage directions, as a *script*; the term *play* will be reserved for the complete performance, or, sometimes, since I do not keep a theatre on my desk, something that I can visualize as a performance while I write. However, my insistence that a play does not become a play until it is produced is not of much help to someone who is studying a 'set play' for an examination and is out of reach of a theatre. The fat section of notes at the back of the book, notes which must be read because questions may be asked on details of the text, but which are often dull reading and supply a wealth of philological, historical and literary information which contributes nothing to the play as a play, is not inspiring. Until

[1] Five of Byron's plays, including *Manfred*, were actually produced in London, and Byron was connected with Drury Lane.

[2] Produced in London with great success in 1713 because of supposed topical interest.

several million more people take a serious interest in the drama, a millenium quite irrelevant to any immediate possibilities, many people will be able to experience drama only through reading and the radio. The radio certainly helps to bring plays to life; but since Shakespeare and the other authors whose plays are normally used as 'set books' did not write for radio, something is lost in an adaptation for this medium. What is the unfortunate examination candidate whose time for awaiting opportunities is limited, or who is hopelessly far away from a suitable theatre, to do?

The best answer I can offer to this question is the answer frequently necessary for apparently insoluble problems; *do it yourself*. Why not? In order to study a play more intelligently and intensively than ever before, try to produce it. No, obviously everyone who has a 'set play' to study cannot produce it; but a team of people, such as one year's class, can very well take part in a production. If there are too few people, it is possible to 'double', that is, to give each person more than one part. In order to 'double' the producer must study the play very carefully to make sure that the person who is playing two parts has time to change from one to the other and to avoid the catastrophe, known to happen in a first run-through, of an unlucky actor trying to be two people at the same time. If, on the other hand, you seem to have far too many people to give everyone something to do—you are mistaken. You will be surprised at how many people can take part in the production of a play; costume-makers, makers-up, electricians, stage hands, makers of properties, researchers to look things up in books, a prompter and people with small special tasks such as ringing a bell at the right time or putting on a record, can all be used. Moreover, in most Shakespeare plays there is scope for non-speaking parts in crowd scenes, and rehearsing these can be very interesting and instructive. It is possible to learn a great deal from a production, too, without having all the resources of the professional theatre at your disposal. A school hall, a classroom, even the open air, will make a primitive theatre, and an audience is generally lenient to faults that are only those of environment.

A lower grade of acting than real production, very useful for students and sometimes more practical than production, because the latter takes a great deal of time and usually a certain amount of money, is the rehearsed play-reading. A properly rehearsed play-reading which can provide an evening's enjoyment very easily and pleasantly. Some properties and improvised costumes may be used.

Lastly, for those who have not even the resources for a rehearsed play-reading, or who, perhaps, have no audience, it is far better at least to read the play aloud with different people taking different parts than for the dialogue never to be spoken at all. If we are asked to read something aloud, we at least have to think what it means, and may for the first time consult the notes and glossary with genuine interest, realizing that without their help we cannot read the part intelligently. True, the standard of reading in this country is rather poor and many of us lack confidence, but the way to improve our standard in any art, and to gain confidence, is to practise it.

These attempts, on varying levels, to treat a play with some respect for the original intentions of the author, are the best way to understand those intentions. We have to understand a line in order to speak it with the proper inflections, or, often, to carry out the action that it implies. In Shakespeare and his contemporaries, whose plays are those most commonly studied for examinations, the stage directions are mostly implied in the dialogue. Indeed, if this is not realized and the directions obeyed, the speech may lose much of its interest.

Prince Henry: Do thou stand for my father, and examine me upon the particulars of my life.

Falstaff: Shall I? content: this chair shall be my state, this dagger my sceptre, and this cushion my crown.

Conventions

Prince Henry:	Thy state is taken for a joint-stool, thy golden sceptre for a leaden dagger, and thy precious rich crown for a pitiful bald crown!
Falstaff:	Well, and the fire of grace be not quite out of thee, now shalt thou be moved. Give me a cup of sack to make my eyes look red, that it may be thought I have wept; for I must speak in passion, and I will do it in King Cambyses' vein.
	(*Drinks*)
Prince Henry:	Well, here is my leg.
Falstaff:	And here is my speech—Stand aside, nobility.
Hostess:	O Jesu, here is excellent sport, i' faith!
Falstaff:	Weep not, sweet Queen, for trickling tears are vain.
Hostess:	O the father, how he holds his countenance!
Falstaff:	For God's sake, lords, convey my tristful queen; for tears do stop the flood-gates of her eyes.

Henry IV, Part I, Act II, Sc. 4

The only stage direction here is 'drinks',[1] but it is clear that much more is required. Falstaff, fat and unwieldy, looks round the room for some suitable properties for his unseemly game. He can easily find something to sit on, and no doubt swings it into place as he mentions it; he can hold up his cheap-looking dagger as a sceptre; but there is nothing in the room that in the least resembles a crown. Perhaps he pauses to look for something. Eventually he picks up a cushion and puts it on his head; by this time all his boon-companions are laughing. He is given his drink, probably by the Hostess, and no doubt takes a good zestful swig, perhaps holding the cushion on to his head as he tilts his head back to swallow the draught. The Prince, on saying, 'Here is my leg,' does not point to his leg; he bows. As soon as Falstaff

---

[1] And we do not know how many of the stage directions in a text of Shakespeare were provided by the original author.

30

So We Must Make It Walk

begins his impersonation he drops into very pompous, affected speech; his imagination concerning the manner of the King is not likely to be accurate and certainly not sympathetic. The Hostess, who has been giggling for some time, is now laughing so much that she has to wipe her eyes, which gives Falstaff a hint for more mock-tragic speech. The words suggest details of gesture—the sweeping movement of gracious dismissal to accompany 'Stand aside, nobility.', the affectionate gesture to the Hostess—perhaps he puts his arm round her if she is near enough—the final gesture to the 'lords' to take the 'queen' away. The make-up expert is told that Falstaff is bald. By the time this has been thought out for a production or play-reading, we have read the script properly.

This scene from a somewhat later play has rather more directions, but the careful reader will see that more happens than is actually indicated by the italicized words. (I have chosen this particular piece because the reader may also like to compare it with the parallel passage in Shakespeare's *Antony and Cleopatra*.)

(*Enter Charmion and Iras.*)

Charmion: What must be done?

Cleopatra: Short ceremony, friends;
But yet it must be decent. First this laurel
Shall crown my hero's head; he fell not basely,
Nor left his shield behind him.—Only thou
Couldst triumph o'er thyself; and thou alone
Wert worthy so to triumph.

Charmion: To what end
These ensigns of your pomp and royalty?

Cleopatra: Dull, that thou art! why, 'tis to meet my love;
As when I saw him first, on Cydnus' bank,
All sparkling, like a goddess: so adorned,
I'll find him once again; my second spousals
Shall match my first in glory. Haste, haste, both,
And dress the bride of Antony.

Charmion: 'Tis done.

Conventions

Cleopatra: Now seat me by my lord. I claim this place;
For I must conquer Caesar too, like him,
And win my share of the world.—Hail, you dear
   relics
Of my immortal love!
O let no impious hand remove you hence:
But rest for ever here! Let Egypt give
His death that peace, which it denied his life—
Reach me the casket.

Iras: Underneath the fruit
The aspic lies.

Cleopatra: Welcome, thou kind deceiver! (*Putting aside the
   leaves*)
Thou best of thieves, who with an easy key
Dost open life, and, unperceived by us,
Even steal us from ourselves; discharging so
Death's dreadful office, better than himself;
Touching our limbs so gentle into slumber,
That Death stands by, deceived by his own
   image,
And thinks himself but sleep.

Serapion: The queen, where is she? (*Within*)
The town is yielded, Caesar at the gates.

Cleopatra: He comes too late to invade the rights of death.
Haste, bare my arm, and rouse the serpent's fury.
   (*Holds out her arm, and draws it back.*)
Coward flesh,
Wouldst thou conspire with Caesar to betray
   me,
As thou wert none of mine? I'll force thee to it,
And not be sent by him,
But bring, myself, my soul to Antony.
   (*Turns aside, and then shows her arm bloody.*)
Take hence; the work is done.

Serapion: Break ope the door, (*Within*)
And guard the traitor well.

Charmion: The next is ours.

So We Must Make It Walk

Iras: Now, Charmion, to be worthy
              Of our great queen and mistress. (*They apply the aspics*.)

Cleopatra: Already, death, I feel thee in my veins:
              I go with such a will to find my lord,
              That we shall quickly meet.
              A heavy numbness creeps through every limb,
              And now 'tis at my head: My eyelids fall
              And my dear love is vanished in a mist.
              Where shall I find him, where? O turn me to him,
              And lay me on his breast!—Caesar, thy worst;
              Now part us, if thou canst. (*Dies*)

                    JOHN DRYDEN: *All For Love*

In this portion of the script we have actual stage directions for the handling of the asps; but the dialogue also implies that Cleopatra places a laurel wreath on the head of the dead Antony; Cleopatra takes up some kind of royal adornments, probably a robe and a crown as in Shakespeare's version, and her maids deck her in her adornments; they lead her to a place beside Antony; and when Cleopatra is dying her maids help her to recline with her head on Antony's breast. Without these actions the words are often almost meaningless. Here is a single speech from a comedy which is certainly not meant to be recited without a good deal of action:

Aimwell: There's something in that which may turn to advantage. The appearance of a stranger in a country church draws as many gazers as a blazing-star; no sooner he comes into the cathedral, but a train of whispers runs buzzing round the congregation in a moment: *Who is he? Whence comes he? Do you know him?* Then I, sir, tips me the verger with half a crown; he pockets the simony, and inducts me to the best pew in church; I pull out my snuff-box, bow to the bishop, or the dean, if he be the commanding officer; single out a beauty, rivet both my eyes to hers, set my nose a-bleeding by

> the strength of imagination, and show the whole
> church my concern, by endeavouring to hide it;
> after the sermon, the whole town gives me to her
> for a lover, and by persuading the lady that I am
> a-dying for her, the tables are turned, and she in
> good earnest falls in love with me.
>
> GEORGE FARQUHAR: *The Beaux' Stratagem*

This does not, like the previous example, necessitate actions
of importance to the development of the play; the function
of the speech is to amuse and to show character; but in production Aimwell would recite this speech with a good deal of
miming of the actions he describes, and with other lively
gestures.

Ophelia's famous mad speech in *Hamlet* presents the producer with many problems:

'There's rosemary, that's for remembrance; pray you,
love, remember; and there's pansies, that's for thoughts. . . .
There's fennel for you, and columbines:—there's rue for
you, and here's some for me:—we may call it herb-grace
o' Sundays:—O, you must wear your rue with a difference.—
There's a daisy: I would give you some violets, but they
wither'd all when my father died;—they say he made a good
end. . . .'

The producer must first find out the language of flowers and
then decide to whom each of these flowers must be given, for
they can all have dramatic significance. Here is a comic
speech from Shakespeare, rather less well known, but worth
studying for the implied stage directions; it would be a good
exercise to work it out in detail and act it:

Launce: Nay 'twill be this hour till I have done weeping; all
this kind of the Launces have this very fault. I have
received my proportion, like the prodigious son,
and am going with Sir Proteus to the imperial's
court. I think Crab my dog be the sourest-natured
dog that lives: my mother weeping, my father wail-
ing, my sister crying, our maid howling, our cat

wringing her hands, and all our house in a great
perplexity, yet did not this cruel-hearted cur shed
one tear: he is a stone, a very pebble-stone, and has
no more pity in him than a dog: a Jew would have
wept to see our parting; why, my grandam, having
no eyes, look you, wept herself blind at my parting.
Nay, I'll show you the manner of it. This shoe is
my father;—no, this left shoe is my father;—no,
no, this left shoe is my mother;—nay, that cannot
be so neither; yes, it is so, it is so,—it hath the
worser sole. This shoe, with the hole in it, is my
mother, and this my father; a vengeance on't! there
'tis: now, sir, this staff is my sister; for look you,
she is as white as a lily, and as small as a wand: this
hat is Nan, our maid: I am the dog: no, the dog is
himself, and I am the dog,—O, the dog is me, and I
am myself; ay, so, so. Now come I to my father;
'Father, your blessing!' now should not the shoe
speak a word for weeping: now should I kiss my
father; well, he weeps on. Now come I to my
mother;—O that she could speak like a wood
woman!—well, I kiss her; why, there 'tis; here's
my mother's breath up and down. Now come I to
my sister; mark the moan she makes. Now the dog
all this while sheds not a tear, nor speaks a word:
but see how I lay the dust with my tears.

Two Gentlemen of Verona, Act II, Sc. 3

Shakespeare has portrayed Launce as a man of very limited
intelligence; but to act his part properly no small amount of
intelligence and application is required.

Modern playwrights use rather more stage directions in
their scripts, so that it is perhaps easier to grasp the significance of a modern play in a silent reading of the script; but
also in studying a contemporary play production throws
much fresh light on the play. For instance, in T. S. Eliot's
The Cocktail Party people are eating and drinking in the

first scene during the conversation and Edward, the host, is moving about the room serving drinks and food until one of the guests tells him he is fussing too much. In production the producer has to see that Edward does give the impression of fussy movement, but does not pass in front of someone who is just speaking, distract attention from important lines or find himself at an impossible angle in relation to someone to whom he has to speak. All this demands detailed concentration.

Thus anything which makes drama really walk and talk is helpful to our appreciation of drama. It is also worth while to mention that to produce a 'set play', give a rehearsed reading of it or even read it aloud with different people in the different parts, adds greatly to the enjoyment of examination work; and alas, examination work can sometimes be made so dull as to destroy the cultural value, the delight in learning, which is the legitimate reason for having schools and colleges and examinations at all. Amateur dramatic societies provide very interesting and worth-while experience for many people whose creativeness cannot go much further than the interpretation of someone else's original creative work. I should like to see the habit of reading plays aloud for fun become popular in English homes; it is more interesting and satisfying than watching the television every evening, because it is more fun to be doing something than to be spoon-fed all the time. The enjoyment of an art is never really a completely passive thing; some co-operation with the artist is always required; and to read a play in the family circle is a very pleasant experience.

An absurd memory I have long cherished may be a dreadful warning against the kind of disproportion and misunderstanding that may arise out of a too passive attitude to drama. Before the war, when I was rather too young to be allowed to comment on the silliness of many grown-up people, I was given a copy of R. E. Sherwood's fine anti-war and anti-Fascist play, *Idiot's Delight*. The play dates rather badly now, but when it was written it was an exciting and

36

So We Must Make It Walk

intelligent warning against the danger of war from European Fascism, and it also contains some interesting characters. My father, my mother and I spent two or three very interesting and instructive evenings reading the play together, sitting at the kitchen table over our one copy and doubling dreadfully, but thoroughly enjoying ourselves; my mother surprised me by being a great success as an enigmatic vamp! Some weeks later a Nonconformist parson visited us. My father, who had been much impressed by *Idiot's Delight*, lent the play to him and asked for his opinion on it, thinking, of course, that a fairly cultured and thoughtful man would get quite an intellectual thrill out of a play with an urgent political theme. The parson read the play, in which on a few occasions someone offers a companion a drink as a social gesture, and when he handed it back to my father my father said, 'How did you like that terrific irony in the last scene?' 'Isn't all that cocktail-drinking dreadful?' said the parson; and the whole family could not extract any other comment from him. So much for silent reading.

III. VISIBLE ACTION

My gentle Reader, I perceive
How patiently you've waited,
And now I fear that you expect
Some tale will be related.

WORDSWORTH: Simon Lee

THE plot of a play, like that of a novel, a short story, or even a narrative poem, is the actual story. It is generally a mechanical exercise to summarize such a story, and a more interesting exercise to study the skill of its construction. In a play, however, both the outline and the details of the plot are governed very largely by this key fact of the three-dimensional nature of drama; the plot must be of a kind that can mostly be represented by ordinary human beings on a public stage.

It is also necessary for the plot of the play to be very clear, so that the audience has no difficulty in following it at the necessary speed; so the plot of a play is generally either a very simple story or one, as in some comedies, in which, though the action is very complicated, enjoyment depends more on seeing the rush of complications than on an appreciation of the full significance of all of them.

An example of the very simple plot is the *Oedipus Rex* of Sophocles. The whole story, if we are asked to summarize it, is: Thebes is stricken by pestilence and therefore a search is made for the murderer of the late king, Laius, lest the land be under a curse because of this unexpiated crime. King Oedipus, who came to Thebes as a stranger some years ago, saved the people from the Sphinx, a monster, and was rewarded with the hand of the widowed queen and the crown, is accused of this crime by the blind prophet Tiresias. Having a clear conscience, he is very angry, and quarrels with the

Visible Action

prophet and with the queen's brother, Creon, accusing them of plotting against him. It does, however, begin to seem possible that he may unknowingly have killed Laius in self-defence. In seeking evidence to prove his innocence, he accidentally finds incontrovertible proof that he killed Laius, that Laius was his own father and that he is now married to his own mother. The horrified queen kills herself; Oedipus puts out his own eyes in a frenzy of horror and despair. This plot is about as simple as a plot can be; there are no side-issues to complicate the one tragic process of discovery. The plot of *Antigone*, already described, is somewhat more complicated, with more than one problem, though all the problems are part of the central dilemma of legality versus humanity. In comedy, too, the plot may be extremely simple, as in Ben Jonson's *The Silent Woman* or Shaw's *Candida;* on the whole comic plots are rather more elaborate than tragic plots.

More complicated plots in tragedy are found in *King Lear*, Webster's *The Duchess of Malfi*, or Ford's *The Broken Heart*. In all of these there is a central theme with a subordinate theme or several subordinate themes. Examples of complicated comedy are Vanbrugh's *The Provok'd Wife* and Christopher Fry's *Venus Observed*; farce, in which action is more important than character and the speedy succession of absurd situations more important than brilliant speeches, has usually very complicated plots and it does not seem to matter very much if we cannot follow them perfectly; modern examples of this are Terence Rattigan's *French Without Tears*, or Brandon Thomas's still popular *Charley's Aunt*. Many modern detective dramas provide good examples of the clever handling of complex plots without having any real literary merit.

If we have to study a play for an examination it is certainly quite sensible to write out a summary of the plot. This is one of the few situations in which it may be more helpful to read the script than to see the play or perform it, in that when we read a script we can go at our own pace and turn back if we do not follow something. This is especially true of a Shake-speare play with its large cast and frequent changes of scene. To write out the story of the play is a good test of under-standing and, like a play-reading, though less so, may make us think about the exact meaning of difficult words and phrases.

However, to disentangle the plot of a play from a careful reading, when everything is organized so that an audience can be expected to take it in at a single performance, is no very remarkable achievement and cannot be called really educational. What is interesting and illuminating is to ex-amine the plot itself in a more critical spirit[1] afterwards, to study its construction and to study the even more interesting technique of how it is made 'good theatre'—effective on the stage and appropriate in every detail to this kind of presenta-tion.

A good story—and this applies to the novel as much as to drama—is more than a sequence of events such as we all live in continually. Some particular events of special interest are emphasized by selection; usually they are events that follow from one another, but this is not essential; these episodes are placed in the environment which will give them the greatest possible force and are conveyed to us by the use of vivid description and realistic dialogue in the novel, realistic dialogue and exciting action on the stage. All the little irrele-vancies of real life are omitted. When the loved husband dies, the wife laments, but probably on the stage does not have to deal with the usual exhausting responsibilities of death, such as arranging the funeral, informing relatives and perhaps selling a large house to buy a small one. When the divorced wife and the new wife meet, they probably do not merely nod or perhaps pass the sandwiches as they may be expected to do in a civilized community in real life.

In real life routine and the minor details of life—washing

---

[1] 'Critical', in a book on literature, does not mean only 'fault-finding', but also 'merit-finding'; the latter is, in literature as in life, normally a far more worth-while and instructive occupation.

stockings, shaving, cleaning our nails, getting the fire to burn, not to mention sleeping about seven hours out of the twenty-four and going out to work most days of the year, take far more of our time and energy than such more interesting and vivid activities as making love, creating great art, introspection, serious argument, making vital decisions, and either really enjoying or really suffering—both quite rare human states. We may sacrifice our lives for freedom, but such a sacrifice can occur at most only once in a lifetime and may be the unexpected culmination of a dull life. This change of proportion, however, does not make drama false; we realize from the beginning that a play is going to treat of something special, a crisis, a conflict or a coincidence, such as bears some resemblance to everyday life but is hardly typical of everyday life. Every daily newspaper provides evidence that what interests us is how people behave in a crisis or what the unusual situation is like. Moreover, the crisis, the violent, the sensational, are seldom as far away as they may appear to be; even in my own fairly quiet and sheltered academic life I have already witnessed, and been involved in, several violently dramatic episodes, and it is rare to meet a person in middle life who has not had a few experiences which are dramatic. The routine of life may, of course, be used for dramatic effect; a meal is fairly often taken on the stage, both in tragedy, e.g. the banquet scene in *Macbeth*, and in comedy, e.g. the afternoon tea in *The Importance of Being Earnest*. A social gesture of drinking may, of course, sometimes become highly dramatic poisoning, as at the death of the Queen in *Hamlet*. Routine may also be deliberately used to stress the monotonous nature of someone's work; this is found in the stress on school routine in *Children in Uniform* and some of the office routine in J. B. Priestley's *Cornelius*, but such routine is shown to an audience only in small samples.

Let us look first at what constitutes a good plot for any type of imaginative narrative, and then at what further technique is needed for a good dramatic plot in which the action

41

Conventions

unfolds in a very short time and before the eyes of an audience. Any good plot is closely constructed; that is, no time is wasted and the events follow one another in credible sequence. The credibility of plot is closely related to the type of work; farce need not be as credible as drawing-room comedy; a 'thriller' is not expected to be as true to life as a psychological novel; but all writers must show at least some regard for the usual reactions to events of human beings and the likely results of their actions. The word *inevitability* is perhaps a trifle too popular with critics, but it does denote an extremely important quality of a really good plot. The chain of events should indeed be a chain with interlocking links, not a string of beads threaded at random. Generally the events of the plot all follow naturally from the first event of the play, as in *Macbeth*, *Antony and Cleopatra* or Somerset Maugham's *Sheppey*; if there is a surprise near the end, it must be a conclusion that, on leisured reflection, we feel was possible after all, as in *Candida* or J. B. Priestley's *Bright Shadow*. It is possible that many well-constructed plays have, like detective stories, been 'written backwards'; the playwright has first invented an interesting conclusion and has then planned the events to lead up to it.

The construction of the broad outlines of the plot of a play differs from that of a novel chiefly in its greater simplicity and speed; the general artistic laws of plot development are probably much the same for any aspect of literature. Several formulae to explain these general laws have been devised. A play must have twists and turns to keep interest until the end. It must develop from one crisis to another. The word *crisis*, as a literary term, does not necessarily mean something alarming or distressing, but merely a crisis of interest, an important event—a sense in which a proposal of marriage may be just as much a crisis as an avalanche. The general outline of the plot of a play will be something like this, though of course this has not the universality of a chemical formula; no attempt to reduce art to formulae can ever be wholly successful; it can only be helpful.

Visible Action

1. The CLARIFICATION or introduction. This is the part of the play in which we learn who the chief characters are, what they are there for and what are the problems with which they start.
2. Some startling development giving rise to new problems. We may call this the FIRST CRISIS.
3. This first crisis will lead on to other actions, events or modifications of character which may in their turn have new consequences carrying the play further forward. Probably the whole plot now proceeds for some time from crisis to crisis. The crises may succeed one another as causes and effects, or some fresh crisis may arise from another cause. This may be called the COMPLICATION.[1]
4. The whole action is brought to a close by some final discovery, action or decision. This is called the DÉNOUE-MENT (untying of the knot).[1]

Let us examine briefly a tragedy, a comedy and a good modern drama in the light of this general formula.

In *Macbeth* the first two scenes provide most of the Clarification; we learn that there are three Witches who plot evil with Macbeth as a tool, that a battle has just taken place and Macbeth has distinguished himself, and that Duncan, a gracious and admired personality, is the King of Scotland. The first crisis comes in the next scene, when the Witches greet the so far noble Macbeth with the promise that he 'shall be king hereafter!' As he is not the legal heir to the throne this leaves him, and the audience, wondering how this can be fulfilled. The prediction works upon the minds of the warrior and his ambitious wife until it brings about the second crisis, the murder of Duncan, an act setting Macbeth irrevocably on the path of crime. This leads to the third crisis of the murder of Banquo, a fourth crisis when the ghost of Banquo appears at the feast and a fifth crisis when Macbeth, having consulted the Witches again, decides upon the murder of Macduff and allows the murder of the latter's

[1] Aristotle uses these terms in a somewhat different sense.

43

helpless wife and children. The dreadfully natural conse-
quence of each evil deed is a further hardening in crime;
Macbeth begins by killing his King, who has a further claim
on his loyalty as his guest; but he goes on to kill a friend and
ends by killing defenceless and harmless strangers; also
most of us will probably feel that his later use of hired assas-
sins is worse than his early murder by his own skill and
strength. Thus though the events are highly sensational, they
are not psychologically improbable. The dénouement comes
in the last battle, when the Witches' prophecies about Bir-
nam Wood and the nature of the man who should defeat
Macbeth come true and the tyrant is killed. The play then
ends quickly with the acknowledgement of the rightful king.
Macbeth is probably one of the best of Shakespeare's plays
from the point of view of construction; we cannot fail to be
impressed by the way in which each evil deed carries its own
consequences of new fears and extended evil. It is an intensification of life, but not unlike life. Indeed, when I was studying the play intensively I was struck by the parallels in the
careers of Macbeth and Hitler; and the parallel held good
even to the final consulting of soothsayers and the wretched
end.

Plot, however, is not Shakespeare's strongest quality. It is
disagreeable to have to find fault with a writer I have long
loved and studied closely and of whom I never tire; but the
student who is just beginning the serious study of Shakespeare needs to be warned that in some ways he is a much
greater artist than craftsman. It is sometimes disconcerting
to look for such virtues of the careful playwright as logical
structure of plot, diligent preservation of the probabilities
of human reaction and character, historical accuracy, or
consistency of detail, in Shakespeare. I can imagine someone
reading this little book, with its deliberate simplifications and
generalizations, as a guide to the study of Shakespeare, and
being much mystified by the many exceptions to the 'rules'
of good play-writing to be found in his works. Shakespeare's
great contemporaries also furnish plenty of exceptions; Ben

Jonson, not the most imaginative, was probably the most careful craftsman.

This is partly because genius is often careless in its wonderful exuberance; but there are also historical reasons, which I will hint at, though this must be very much simplified. In England the craft of the drama was still in a somewhat primitive state while the art of the drama—the rich imagination, wide sympathies and fluent poetry—was having one of the greatest flowerings in literary history. In France three of the greatest dramatists, Corneille, Molière and Racine, wrote at a time when the craft of the drama was much discussed and there were severe, often over-severe, critics to demand a high standard in detail. The French drama is no more impressive than Shakespeare, though no less so; sometimes it seems less human and spontaneous, though more logical and dignified; but one never feels the need to make excuses for Racine as one sometimes must for Shakespeare. As far as I am concerned Shakespeare is very welcome to do as he pleases until his debunkers do better; even Shaw, one of few conscious and deliberate rivals, did not excel him in variety and imagination, though in intellect perhaps he did. Idolators of Shakespeare sometimes claim to see brilliant touches of truth and nature in oddities which were perhaps only the carelessnesses of a busy man; this is partly the result of the habit of reading Shakespeare silently instead of performing him or seeing him performed; a play-reading very soon shows where the speeches are clumsy or the characters lack conviction, just as it brings out the magnificent dramatic power of the best scenes and the complex fascination of the greatest characters. To treat Shakespeare as perfect in every way is as stupid and misleading as to patronize him.

The plots of Shakespeare's comedies generally have faults of construction; a better example of construction in comedy may be found in Ben Jonson's *Volpone*. In this play the Clarification extends right over Act I: we learn that the clever and callous cynic Volpone is making a fortune by pretending to be near death, so that avaricious people, Voltore, Corbaccio, Corvino and Lady Politick Would-be, bring him valuable presents in the hope that he will think them true friends and make them his heirs. He is helped in this conspiracy by his servant Mosca. The Clarification is itself very amusing, with its variations on the same theme; a hint of further development is given when Mosca suggests successfully, that Corbaccio should disinherit his good son Bonario in favour of Volpone, in order to give the latter an overwhelming proof of his devotion.

The first Crisis comes when Volpone is seized with a sudden and evil passion for the gentle and honourable Celia, wife of Corvino. Mosca persuades Corvino to offer even his wife to Volpone in the hope of wealth, and a second crisis comes when Bonario indignantly rescues her from this vile situation. To save themselves the avaricious legacy-hunters conspire to bear false witness against the innocent pair; this leads to an exciting court scene in which Celia and Bonario are condemned. The complication now develops into a fourth crisis; Volpone pretends to be dead and Mosca to be his heir, in order that they may enjoy the mortification of the legacy-hunters. The latter are suitably infuriated, but a further twist brings about the dénouement; Mosca tries to keep the fortune for himself by insisting that his master is really dead, and in a final court scene in which the intrigue moves very fast Volpone confesses and brings down punishment on his own head as well as on Mosca and the legacy-hunters.

A well-constructed modern comedy is J. M. Barrie's *What Every Woman Knows*. The clarification is very short; we see a father and two brothers very sympathetically discussing the inability of their much-loved sister Maggie to find a husband. They are very fond of her and anxious to do all they can for her. When the sister comes in we also learn that the men are very conscious of their lack of education and that they are sitting up in the hope of catching a burglar who has already been in the house twice. Presently the 'burglar' comes in and proves to be a harmless but odd young man,

Visible Action

John Shand, who is ambitious and uses the house in order to study. The First Crisis, a very unexpected one, comes when the brothers offer him a bargain: he can have three hundred pounds to further his education if, Maggie being still unmarried at the end of five years, he will marry her, provided that she is willing. Eventually John accepts the offer. In Act II we learn that John has been elected as a Member of Parliament and is obviously on the way to success. Six years have passed, for Maggie, who has come to love him, did not want to hinder him; but now he knows that he ought to fulfil his part of the bargain. The second crisis comes when Maggie, who is painfully conscious of what she thinks is her own inadequacy to be the wife of a man with great prospects, bravely offers to release him after a long struggle with herself. John is tempted, but sticks to his side of the bargain. The next crisis is of a different kind. Maggie and John are married and she is being very much more useful to him in such matters as polishing speeches than he realizes; but after we have been given dramatic and amusing evidence of her value in promoting his interests we are shown how John has fallen in love—a rather unreal love —with the beautiful and attractive young Lady Sybil Tenterden. Maggie, who overhears some of the love scene, forces John's hand and he makes a public declaration of his passion for Sybil, who is prepared to suffer disgrace for his sake. Maggie arranges that John shall spend the next three weeks at the house of a friend and in the company of Sybil. John thinks it is Sybil who helps and inspires him, but in Act IV we learn that the speech he has prepared in Maggie's absence is not a good one. There is a rapid and very amusing dénouement when it is revealed, first that three weeks of each other's company has made John and Sybil tired of one another and they realize their great passion was only calf-love; that Maggie's altered version of John's speech is brilliant and will be the making of his career; and, in the touching final moments of the play, that Maggie has won John's real love and appreciation at last.

Conventions

The careful student would do well to study several more plays, old and new, from the point of view of the broad outlines of the plot structure, but the formula should never be applied too rigidly, nor should any student make the mistake of thinking that a play which does not fit it is a bad play. There are many variations on this structure. One, used only in modern times, so far as I know, is the 'flash-back' in which the chronological sequence of events is altered so that we see first a situation and then some of the circumstances which led up to it; this is found in Bridie's *It Depends What You Mean*, Priestley's *Time and the Conways* and Noel Coward's *The Astonished Heart*. There are other variations on the general formula.

There is usually little difficulty in disentangling the main plot of a play with its Clarification, First Crisis, Complication and Dénouement; but many good plays have a sub-plot, or several sub-plots, or occasionally two parallel plots of approximately equal importance, to complicate the action further, add interest or give relief. A sub-plot which complicates the action further and intensifies rather than relieving the tension is to be found in *King Lear*, where the sufferings of Lear at the hands of his wicked daughters and the goodness of the loyal Cordelia are paralleled by the adventures of Gloucester and his two sons, one good, one bad. In this play the two plots are closely connected and affect each other. A sub-plot that does not further the main action and simply adds interest is the comic courtship of Touchstone and Audrey in *As You Like It*, an episode which has a unity of its own, though at the end of the play this comic couple joins the queue to be married. An example of a sub-plot that provides emotional relief and contrast is the courtship of Benedick and Beatrice in *Much Ado About Nothing*; this lively relationship, with wit-combats developing into adult comradeship, helps us to accept a rather inadequate happy ending to the tale of Hero, which could easily be tragic and is, indeed, at its supreme crisis, treated

48

Visible Action

tragically. Indeed, in this play it is difficult to tell which is
meant to be the more important of the two plots. This kind
of contrast is even more marked in the 'heroic plays' of the
seventeenth century, in which, perhaps as a reaction against
the dreariness of the Puritan régime, playwrights sought to
tickle the palates of their audiences with very strong sensations and often heightened these by contrast. For instance,
Dryden's *Don Sebastian* has a main plot, with speeches in
blank verse, of great sensationalism and overflowing with
impossible pride and improbable magnanimities. The prose
sub-plot is comic and somewhat coarse. A good exercise
for a student would now be to take the three plots of *A Midsummer Night's Dream* (the Fairies, the Lovers and the
Rustics) and work out how these are combined to make one
brilliant complication leading to a satisfying dénouement.
The student will notice how in this play the dénouement is
longer than usual, because there are so many complications
to be unravelled.

The plot of a tragedy is generally more important than
that of a comedy, in the sense that the changes wrought in
the fortunes of various people are greater and more irre-
vocable. Until recently, tragedy nearly always ended with
the death of one or more of the principal characters, as in all
Shakespeare's tragedies. This is probably because death is
the only final disaster, especially to unimaginative minds. If
we consider the matter rationally, it is perhaps absurd to see
death as a catastrophe, for we know that we must all die
some day and sometimes, as in *King Lear* or *Antony and
Cleopatra*, the actual death of the hero or heroine is good
rather than ill fortune. But the tradition is firm, though I
have sometimes wondered whether it may not one day be
possible to write a comedy that ends with a happy death.
Somerset Maugham has come near to this in *Sheppey*, and
in his very grim play *For Services Rendered* the suicide of one
character is not as distressing as the continued life of the
woman who is in love with him, who after a fit of uncontrol-
lable grief becomes insane. The tragic ending, often truer to

49

real life,[1] of people having to go on struggling with a wretched existence, is more common nowadays than it used to be, but it is still not the most usual tragic ending, perhaps because it is very difficult to handle without a sense of anti-climax. Examples of this treatment may be found in a fairly mild form in Chekov's *The Three Sisters* and in a much grimmer form in Ibsen's *Ghosts*, Lilian Hellman's *The Children's Hour*, Terence Rattigan's *The Browning Version*[2] and still more his *The Deep Blue Sea*, perhaps one of the most truly tragic of modern prose plays. Somerset Maugham's *The Letter* begins with a death, but the real tragedy of this play is that a woman is left, having killed the man she loved, to live in disgrace with a husband she cannot love.

The plot of a comedy may be altogether slighter, though it frequently concludes with a marriage or marriages. This, like death in tragedy, is largely a convention of finality. In comedy the atmosphere is so much less serious that we are temporarily prepared to believe that the most incongruous marriages will be successful: Claudio, who has cruelly disgraced her in public, is to make Hero happy in *Much Ado About Nothing*; the noble Celia is entrusted to the too newly penitent Oliver in *As You Like It*; the marriage and reconciliation of Bertram and Helena in *All's Well that Ends Well* is really shocking, Bertram being the most contemptible young man in Shakespeare. Paulina and Camillo in *The Winter's Tale* are both good people, but there is little guarantee that their hasty marriage, an obvious tying up of a loose end, will work. There is a convention in both drama and fiction that a marriage which comes at the end of the story is going to be a happy one, though there have always been literary treatments, serious or humorous, of unhappy marriages in the body of a play or novel.

[1] At least in Christian civilizations, where suicide is regarded as a sin.

[2] The film version of this play has a strong dénouement which is more satisfying emotionally, though less true to normal life.

Visible Action

Coincidence may be used by a dramatist, in both tragedy and comedy, with little regard to mathematical probabilities, though good artists try to achieve at least the appearance of possibility; but the heightening of real life is not necessarily a distortion, and most of us can think of a few coincidences in our own lives which would strike us as far-fetched if we met them in a book. What looks like pure chance does play a very considerable part in human life, in such things as the finding of a mate, the choice of a career, the state of bodily health and even such more inward things as our moral and spiritual values, which cannot but be, in part, the creation of our early environment.[1] Up to a point verisimilitude of plot does not much matter so long as it convinces us at the time; a particularly startling and almost comic example of this is Webster's *The Duchess of Malfi*, in which a very improbable and melodramatic plot is given most of the quality of great tragedy by the magnificent poetry and the force of the characterization. Gross inconsistency in character displeases the intelligent spectator far more than an unlikely plot, for whereas almost anything can happen in human life, very sudden changes of character are rare and unconvincing.

So much for the broad outlines of plot construction. It is not possible to reduce the details even to a vague formula, but it may be possible to throw some light on the details by the use of examples. In a play the action must all be either visible to the audience, or made convincing by a relation of the events recited on the stage. In Greek tragedy deaths do not occur in view of the audience, but a messenger relates an account of them and afterwards the bodies are shown to us to add conviction. The classicist tragedy of Racine also avoids violent action on the stage; but there is no lack of very violent emotion to make the play interesting. However action is treated, the audience must be made to believe in it for the period of the performance.

The details of the clarification usually show great dramatic

[1] Or perhaps the result of a revolt against an early environment, in which case they are still, to some extent, conditioned.

craftsmanship; indeed, it is possible that they are the supreme test of such craftsmanship. For in the first few minutes of the play the audience must be put in possession of the problem, or most of the problem, and of at least some of the characters. To do all this in a few minutes is by no means easy.

In *King Lear* the very first scene arouses keen interest and leaves the audience in suspense. First we are introduced to Gloucester and his two sons, in language which leaves us in no doubt of their relationship and encourages us to expect trouble from Edmund later; then we are immediately plunged into the critical scene of the division of the kingdom. By the end of one scene we have a very clear idea of the characters of Lear, Cordelia, Goneril, Regan, Kent, Gloucester, Edmund, the King of France and the Duke of Burgundy; and the division of the kingdom is obviously going to lead to further crises.

After a few lines of epigram, Congreve's *The Way of the World* opens thus:

Fainall: Prithee, why so reserv'd? Something has put you out of Humour.

Mirabell: Not at all; I happen to be grave to Day; and you are gay; that's all.

Fainall: Confess, Millamant and you quarrelled last Night, after I left you; my fair Cousin has some Humours that would tempt the Patience of a Stoick. What some Coxcomb came in, and was well receiv'd by her, while you were by.

Mirabell: Witwoud, and Petulant; and what was worse, her Aunt, your Wife's Mother, my evil Genius; or to sum up all in her own Name, my old Lady Wishfort came in.—

Fainall: O there it is then.—She has a lasting Passion for you, and with Reason.—What, then, my Wife was there?

Mirabell: Yes, and Mrs. Marwood and three or four more,

whom I never saw before; seeing me, they all put on their grave Faces, whisper'd one another; then complained aloud of the Vapours, and after fell into a prolong'd Silence.

Fainall: They had a mind to be rid of you.

Mirabell: For which good reason I resolv'd not to stir. At last the good old Lady broke through her painful Taciturnity, with an Invective against long Visits. I would not have understood her, but Millamant joining in the Argument, I rose and with a constrain'd Smile told her, I thought nothing was so easie as to know when a Visit began to be troublesome; she reden'd and I withdrew, without expecting her to reply.

Fainall: You were to blame to resent what she spoke only in Compliance with her Aunt.

Mirabell: She is more Mistress of herself, than to be under the necessity of such a Resignation.

Fainall: What? though half her Fortune depends upon her marrying with my Lady's Approbation?

Mirabell: I was then in such a Humour, that I should have been better pleas'd if she had been less discreet.

Fainall: Now I remember, I wonder not they were weary of you; last Night was one of their Cabal-Nights; they have 'em three times a Week, and meet by turns, at one another's Apartments, where they come together like the Coroner's Inquest, to sit upon the murder'd Reputations of the Week. You and I are excluded; and it was once propos'd that all the Male Sex should be excepted; but some body mov'd that to avoid Scandal there might be one Man of the Community; upon which Witwoud and Petulant were enroll'd Members.

Mirabell: And who may have been the Foundress of this Sect? My Lady Wishfort, I warrant, who publishes her Detestation of Mankind; and full of the Vigour of Fifty five, declares for a Friend and

Ratafia;[1] and let Posterity shift for itself, she'll breed no more.

Fainall: The Discovery of your sham Addresses to her, to conceal your Love to her Niece, has provok'd this Separation: Had you dissembled better, Things might have continued in the State of Nature.

The group of women who meet for spiteful conversation has been used elsewhere in literature; we are reminded of the Collegiate Ladies in *The Silent Woman*, the vicious gossip in Clare Booth's *The Women* and especially the ladies in *The School for Scandal*. Here a sensible man's complaints of this spiteful clique give opportunities for the problem of the play to be stated; we learn that Mirabell loves Millamant, but is hindered in his courtship by the fact that Lady Wishfort, Millamant's guardian, can deprive Millamant of half her fortune if she makes an unauthorized marriage; and, though there seems to be nothing undesirable about Mirabell, Lady Wishfort is not likely to approve such a marriage, in that she wants him for herself. We also hear of several of the other characters, who will play an important part in the coming intrigues. Thus, in a spirited dialogue, the audience is placed in possession of a number of vital facts and a state of gleeful expectation is ensured.

An outstanding beginning for a modern tragedy is that of Terence Rattigan's *The Deep Blue Sea*. First a pleasant young couple appears, then the caretaker-housekeeper of a block of flats and lastly a doctor who is not on the register— thus arousing immediate interest in a mysterious character. Hester Collyer, the heroine, is just saved from committing suicide by gas on top of an overdose of aspirin. For several minutes at the beginning of the play we have the fast-moving and suspense-filled action of the rescue. As soon as Hester is known to be physically safe and there is a chance of a release

[1] Not the biscuit, but a liqueur which was then fashionable.

of tension the tension is maintained by a dramatic revelation; her legal husband, who is telephoned, is not the man she has been living with and is, incidentally, a public figure of some distinction. The opportunities for development here are magnificent, and this powerful tragedy of a passionate woman obsessively in love with someone who cannot return her intensity of passion is a play in which the emotional tension is never released. The climax of the play, in which the ruined doctor forces Hester to face her tragedy, too, so that she can refrain from committing suicide, is almost unbearable.

The clarification as handled by a less skilled playwright unmercifully reveals his inadequacies. The beginning of Henry Jones's *The Earl of Essex* (1791) is an example of the heavy and clumsy imparting of information to be found at the beginning of a bad play:

Burleigh: The bill, at length, has pass'd opposing numbers,
While crowds seditious clamour'd round the
    senate,
And headlong faction urg'd its force within.

Raleigh: It has, my lord—The wish'd for day is come,
When this proud idol of the people's hearts
Shall now no more be worshipp'd.—Essex falls.
My lord, the minute's near that shall unravel
The mystic schemes of this aspiring man.
Now fortune, with officious hand, invites us
To her, and opens wide the gates of greatness,
The way to power. My heart exults; I see,
I see, my lord, our utmost wish accomplish'd!
I see great Cecil shine without a rival,
And England bless him as her guardian saint.
Such potent instruments I have prepar'd,
As shall, with speed, o'erturn this hated man,
And dash him down, by proof invincible.

Burleigh: His day of glory now is set in night,
And all my anxious hopes at last are crown'd.
These proofs against him, Raleigh—

55

Conventions

Raleigh: All arrived.
Burleigh: Arrived! how? when?
Raleigh: This very hour, my lord:
           Nay more, a person comes, of high distinction,
           To prove some secret treaties made by Essex,
           With Scotland's monarch, and the proud Tyrone.
Burleigh: How say'st? to prove 'em?
Raleigh: Ay, my lord, and back'd
           With circumstances of a stronger nature.
           It now appears, his secretary Cuff,
           With Blunt and Lee, were deep concern'd in this
           Destructive scheme, contriv'd to raise this lord
           And ruin Cecil. O, it is a subtile,
           A deep-laid mischief, by the earl contriv'd,
           In hour malignant, to o'erturn the state,
           And (horror to conceive!) dethrone the queen.

This might be a little livelier if it were not written in bad blank verse; as it is it is so heavy as to be almost comical. A great play whose clarification is its weakest point is Shakespeare's *Henry V*.

A dramatic device which greatly heightens the emotional intensity of a play is contrast. The Porter at the Gate in *Macbeth*, as De Quincey pointed out, shows us the rough, normal workaday world intruding upon a scene of almost unnatural horror and so heightens the horror. The terrible ending of Sean O'Casey's *Juno and the Paycock* is made more terrible by the final comic dialogue of the worthless, lazy husband and his boon companion Joxer, which follows immediately on a tragic prayer spoken by Juno Boyle before she leaves the house for ever with her broken-hearted and betrayed daughter. The squalid humour makes the suffering seem more real by contrast and also confirms our sense of the inevitability of the tragedy by once again showing Boyle's incompetence as head of the family. In John L. Balderston's *Berkeley Square*, a play on the theme of travelling in time, the contrasts between the manners of the eigh-

Visible Action

teenth century and the really more refined manners of the twentieth is continually stressed; the strength of this play comes from the fact that the central character, Peter Standish, remains the same in two vividly contrasting worlds. *She Stoops to Conquer* is full of comic contrasts: in the first scene Mrs. Hardcastle is talking of her delicate son Tony and his intellectual promise; having had a brief glimpse of Tony as neither delicate nor intelligent, we next see him singing and shouting in the alehouse; later, young Marlowe's bluff manner when he mistakes the house for an inn is useful not only for its intrinsic comicality but for emphasizing, by contrast, his bashfulness when confronted with a well-bred girl, whom he meets with a bold face when he thinks she is a barmaid.

Surprise is an important element in the plot of both a novel and a play, but in a play it may be more forcefully effective, since we actually see the reactions of other people to it. The persons of the play only may be surprised, because the audience is in the secret already, as in the plays of Shakespeare where the audience know that a boy is often a girl in disguise, and in *Oedipus Rex* or the *Agamemnon* of Aeschylus, in which the story was already very well known to the audience; but the audience may also be startled, as in Ben Jonson's *The Silent Woman*, in which the woman proves unexpectedly to be a boy in disguise, Somerset Maugham's *The Sacred Flame*, in which we are kept guessing about the identity of a murderer, though this is not primarily a detective play but a problem play, and J. B. Priestley's *Laburnum Grove*, in which a dull suburban business-man proves to be a large-scale crook engaged in counterfeiting, which he confesses in a quiet conversation over the supper table. Later we are made to think that this was just a device to tease the family and test the daughter's spineless fiancé. Near the end of the play we learn that the story is true. The three surprises are very well timed.

A trick which the novelist is not able to use is that of significant silence. One of the most effective examples of

this is to be found in Chekov's *The Cherry Orchard*. In the
script it may not be noticed, but on the stage it is unforgettable. The charming but wayward Madame Ranevsky is
ruined and has to sell her estate, including her beloved
cherry orchard; she has an opportunity to save the rest of
the estate if she will cut the orchard down and use the land
for building; she cannot bear to do this, because the orchard
symbolizes her happier past; but the orchard is sold by
auction and Lopakhin, a man descended from serfs, buys it;
in Madame Ranevsky's presence, not from cruelty but from
excitement, he gloats over his new purchase and his plans for
cutting down the trees. We have previously seen Madame
Ranevsky as pathetically lively, volatile and talkative; now
we see her perfectly silent and motionless all through
Lopakhin's long speech; later she weeps, but still says
nothing; others speak to her sympathetically, but she remains silent till the curtain falls. An example of dramatically
effective silence which will be familiar to all readers of this
book is in *Hamlet*, Act I, Sc. 2, in which the hero maintains
a grim silence throughout the polite speeches and stately
ceremonies, and, when addressed, is as taciturn as he dare
be, pouring out his suppressed emotion only when he is left
alone. Dramatic irony or the double meaning is a popular
device for intensifying the reactions of the audience, in both
tragedy and comedy. A character on the stage says something which has one meaning to him and sometimes to the
other people present, but quite another possible meaning
to the audience and sometimes to another person on the
stage. The numerous disguises in Shakespeare's comedies
give abundant scope for this, as when, in *As You Like It*,
Rosalind, disguised as a man and trying to live up to her
part, faints at the sight of blood and is told, 'You lack a
man's heart'. *The Comedy of Errors*, with its two sets of
identical twins, consists almost entirely of talk at cross-
purposes owing to mistaken identity. There is tragic irony in
Romeo and Juliet when Romeo believes Juliet to be dead and
kills himself in despair, though the audience knows that she

Visible Action

is only drugged and Romeo himself comments on the absence of any of the changes wrought by death. *Macbeth* and *Hamlet* are full of irony; the reader should be able to collect examples from these plays. There are many conversations at cross-purposes in the plays of Noel Coward; Terence Rattigan's *Who is Sylvia?* is a modern comedy in which misunderstandings that have an ironical effect play an important part. Another and very famous example of this kind of thing is the screen scene in *The School for Scandal*. Irony of situation is by no means out of the reach of the novelist, being frequently found in Hardy, Fielding, Thackeray and Somerset Maugham, but the ironies of drama are more emphatic, partly because we actually see them and partly because, like everything in the drama, their effect is concentrated by brevity.

One of the special technical difficulties that faces the dramatist is the handling of material that is essential to the plot but that cannot all be conveniently shown on the stage. This can be done very badly or very well. The use of the Messenger in the Greek tragedies is an example of the skilled communication of such information, because the Messenger is given a fine speech and can do much to convey his own feelings and reactions. The same method of communicating what could certainly not be shown on the stage is found in Milton's *Samson Agonistes*, a play modelled on the Greek methods and perfectly capable of being performed, though it was not written with that intention:

Messenger: Occasions drew me early to this City,
                And as the gates I enter'd with Sun-rise,
                The morning Trumpets Festival proclaim'd
                Through each high street: little I had dispatch't
                When all abroad was rumour'd that this day
                Samson should be brought forth to shew the people
                Proof of his mighty strength in feats and games;
                I sorrow'd at his captive state, but minded

Conventions

Not to be absent at that spectacle.
The building was a spacious Theatre
Half round on two main Pillars vaulted high,
With seats where all the Lords and each degree
Of sort, might sit in order to behold,
The other side was op'n, where the throng
On banks and scaffolds under Skie might stand;
I among these aloof obscurely stood.
The Feast and noon grew high, and Sacrifice
Had fill'd their hearts with mirth, high cheer and
    wine,
When to their sports they turn'd. Immediately
Was *Samson* as a public servant brought,
In their state Livery clad; before him Pipes
And Timbrels, on each side went armed guards,
Both horse and foot before him and behind
Archers, and Slingers, Cataphracts and Spears.
At sight of him the people with a shout
Rifted the Air clamouring their god with praise,
Who had made their dreadful enemy thir thrall.
He patient but undaunted where they led him,
Came to the place, and what was set before him
Which without help of eye, might be assay'd,
To heave, pull, draw, or break, he still per-
    form'd
All with incredible, stupendous force,
None daring to appear Antagonist.
At length for intermission sake they led him
Between the pillars; he his guide requested
(For so from such as nearer stood we heard)
As over-tir'd to let him lean a while
With both his arms on those two massie Pillars
That to the arched roof gave main support.
He unsuspitious led him; which when *Samson*
Felt in his arms, with head a while declin'd,
And eyes fast fixt he stood, as one who pray'd,
Or some great matter in his mind revolv'd.

60

Visible Action

At last with head erect thus cryed aloud,
Hitherto, Lords, what your commands impos'd
I have perform'd, as reason was, obeying,
Not without wonder or delight beheld.
Now of my own accord such other tryal
I mean to shew you of my strength, yet greater;
As with amaze shall strike all who behold.
This utter'd, straining all his nerves he bow'd,
As with the force of winds and waters pent,
When Mountains tremble, those two massie
    Pillars
With horrible convulsion to and fro,
He tugg'd, he shook, till down they came and
    drew
The whole roof after them, with burst of thunder
Upon the heads of all who sate beneath,
Lords, Ladies, Captains, Councellors, or
    Priests.
Thir choice nobility and flower, not only
Of this but each *Philistian* City round
Met from all parts to solemnize this Feast.
Samson with these inmixt, inevitably
Pull'd down the same destruction on himself;
The vulgar only scap'd who stood without.

This is about as long a single speech as a play will stand, but if it is ably spoken and the other people on the stage react suitably it is very impressive. The reader may like to compare the more violent and colloquial account of a terrible sight given by the Chaplain in Shaw's *Saint Joan*, in which the burning of the saint is described by a man hysterical with horror.

Letters are often used on the stage as a means of conveying information quickly and neatly. In Farquhar's *The Constant Couple* Colonel Standard brings back to Sir Harry Wildair his letters once written to Lady Lurewell, to tell him that he is no longer loved, and the Colonel gloats and chuckles over the hero's discomfiture. However, the Colonel does not know that Harry has also a letter in the packet addressed to himself:

Wildair: Here's a copy of verses too: I must turn poet, the devil's name—Stay—'Sdeath, what's here:—This is her hand—Oh, the charming characters!— (*Reading*)—'My dear Wildair,'—That's I, 'egad! —'This huff-bluff colonel'—that's he—'is the rarest fool in nature,'—the devil he is!—'and as such have I used him.'—with all my heart, faith— 'I had no better way of letting you know that I lodge in St. James, near the holy lamb. Lurewell.' —Colonel, I am your most humble servant.

Standard: Hold, sir, you sha'n't go yet; I ha'n't delivered half my message.

Wildair: Upon my faith but you have, colonel.

Letters are very often used to further the intrigue in Restoration comedy; in Steele's *The Conscious Lovers*, a little later, there are even on one occasion two letters close together in one scene. A use of a letter for a more suitable dramatic purpose is to be found in Terence Rattigan's play of Air Force life during the last war, *Flare Path*. In this very clever play one of the characters is a Polish count whose knowledge of English is so limited that his attempts to speak it are a source of amusement to everyone; he has married an English barmaid. Near the end of the play, when it appears that the Count has been killed, his wife asks a visiting film star to translate a letter he has written to her to have if anything happens to him; he wrote the letter in French, knowing his own inadequacy in English. The film star translates the letter for her and reads it out to her in the beautiful voice of a professional actor. It is a very strongly-worded and sincere declaration of love and provides the most moving moments of the play. Doris, who had doubted her husband's love is assured too late, as it seems; a few minutes later the Count comes in, having fallen into the sea and successfully made

Visible Action

his way back. Immediately he tries to explain himself in his very bad English, and, especially after the suspense, his story is hilariously funny. Only by this masterly device of the translated letter could Mr. Rattigan succeed in making the Polish Count a completely serious character when this seriousness is required. (The whole play is very well worth studying for its plot construction and masterly dramatic technique.)

Another very important aspect of this communication without the action or character being present is to be found in the discussion of characters by other characters; this will be investigated in the chapter on Character. Before this is studied, however, a separate chapter will be given to one special aspect of the plot of a play, an aspect often of great importance to the literary student—the adaptation of a non-dramatic plot for a dramatic work.

IV. ADAPTATION OF PLOTS

'Hoste,' quod I, 'ne beth nat yvel apayd,
For other tale certes can I noon,
But of a ryme I lerned long agoon.'
                    CHAUCER: *Prologue to Sir Thopas*

THE student of a Shakespeare play usually has to give some attention to the 'sources'. Obviously every play has a 'source' in that the plot must have come from somewhere; plots do not happen by accident. Nowadays originality is regarded as a merit much more than in the days of Shakespeare, and on a few occasions has perhaps even been excessively cultivated for its own sake. The modern dramatist generally tries to take a plot from his own head or from some not very well-known episode in history; or, as an alternative, he may show his originality by taking a very old well-known plot, such as a Greek myth or a well-known historical episode and so handling it as to throw a new light upon it.

Examples of the completely original plot, so far as I know, are Stephen Spender's *Trial of a Judge*, J. B. Priestley's *An Inspector Calls*, Čapek's *The Insect Play* and *R.U.R.*, and Shaw's *On the Rocks*. It will be noticed that a love theme predominates in none of these; it would be difficult to think of a play with a love theme which bore no resemblance to the plot of any other play.

Examples of the choice of a relatively little-known episode from the past are John Drinkwater's *Robert E. Lee*, the theme of which is doubtless well known in the United States but unfamiliar to most English readers, Shaw's *Great Catherine*, Laurence Housman's *Pains and Penalties*, or

64

Adaptation of Plots

Terence Rattigan's *The Winslow Boy*. History is a mine of good stories, and as it is continually being made it is never likely to be exhausted. Moreover, with imagination a playwright can create a whole play of passion and conflict out of a very few lines in a history book; it has been said that the entire source for Racine's *Britannicus* was one line of Latin. Whether this is true I do not know, but it certainly could be; any live history book or old chronicle contains dozens of sentences that could be themes for plays.

Examples of the startlingly novel treatment of well-known subjects are: Anouilh's *Point of Departure*, an amazing modernization of the theme of Orpheus and Eurydice; Anouilh's *Antigone*, which was highly topical in relation to the French Resistance Movement; Shaw's *Androcles and the Lion*, *Caesar and Cleopatra* and *In Good King Charles' Golden Days*; Oscar Wilde's *Salome*, in which Salome is shown as physically attracted by John the Baptist; Bridie's *Jonah and the Whale*; Rudolf Besier's *The Barretts of Wimpole Street* with its horrifying psychological theory about the motives of Mr. Barrett; and many of the rather too numerous modern Nativity plays, many of which are embarrassingly sentimental and unworthy of their theme; a respectable specimen of this genre is Dorothy Sayer's *He that Should Come*, and another spirited one is Henri Ghéon's *Christmas in the Market Place*, though I myself find it almost unbearably irritating in structure.

In looking at historical plays we should remember that a play which now seems to be on a hackneyed theme may have been novel when it was written and a play which seemed highly topical when it was written may now have become obscure; for example, few modern dramatists could get away with a play about Henry VIII; the Tudors, as source-material, now need a long rest; but Shakespeare's[1] *Henry VIII* was almost dangerously topical when it was written; Chapman's *Perkin Warbeck* was less remote to the Jacobeans

---

[1] Or Fletcher's, or the work of both dramatists in collaboration; 'there has been much throwing about of brains'.

Conventions

than it is to us; and Dryden's *Amboyna*, now a museum piece, was once up-to-the-minute topicality.

It is often said that there are very few possible plots in the world and that all drama makes use of permutations and combinations of one or more of such themes as: mistaken jealousy, rivalry in love, love versus duty, rivalry for power, honour versus profit, love surmounting family opposition, mistaken identity, lost heirs and so on. This may well be true, but fortunately for the dramatist, though the number of basic human conflicts is rather small, all human beings are different and live in different ways, so that the possible variety of the details of situation is infinite. Moreover, every time drama spreads to a new audience this provides new possibilities, and changes in the structure of society, or in manners and customs, also give scope for new kinds of dramatic treatment. For instance, a whole new Communist drama sprang up after the Russian Revolution and a new propagandist theatre is now developing in Communist China; the spread of drama to schools, because of its immense educational value, gives a new field of drama-for-children, which is often very poor but also includes such excellent works as Robert Graves's charming *Horses*; well-known dramatists such as Lady Gregory, A. A. Milne and Terence Rattigan have written plays for children. The development of interest in Choral Speaking makes possible a revival of drama with a Chorus, such as T. S. Eliot's *Murder in the Cathedral*, and so on. Thus the drama is never likely to be exhausted.

We may think for a moment that nowadays it is not considered honourable to take a plot from some other literary work as Shakespeare did, perhaps keeping even some of the words; but this is not true. What happens nowadays is that the new play is called a *dramatization* or an *adaptation* to distinguish it from a play with a wholly original plot and to give the proper credit to the author of the source-work.[1]

[1] If the author of the source-book is living, of course, his permission must be sought, and a copyright fee paid.

Adaptation of Plots

Everyone who goes to the pictures must be familiar with the credit-title 'From the story by . . . Screenplay by . . .' that appears on the screen at the beginning of such a film. A great many good films and a number of good plays have been dramatizations of novels or short stories. Sometimes this is even done by the original author collaborating with a partner who knows more about the special technique of drama. Innumerable dramatizations of prose fiction are prepared for the radio, and the practice of simple dramatization is gaining ground in schools, where it provides a perfect and very palatable test of comprehension as well as valuable creative exercise. Another form of adaptation is, of course, straight translation from some foreign play that it seems would appeal to an English audience; for instance, Miles Malleson's excellent free translations of Molière have been very successful. Earlier, Henry Fielding translated some of Molière, and the versatile if not inspired Aaron Hill translated several of the tragedies of Voltaire; Ambrose Philips made a version of Racine's *Andromaque* as *The Distrest Mother*, which was once fairly successful; and today Anouilh's plays have been translated into English very soon after their appearance in French.

When a novel is adapted for dramatic purposes the adaptation must conform to the special needs of drama; for instance, it may be necessary to simplify the plot so that it can be taken in at one performance; and it will almost certainly be necessary to contrive various economies of scene. For example, in Helen Jerome's quite sound adaptation of *Pride and Prejudice* two of the five daughters, the studious Mary and the silly Kitty, are omitted for the sake of simplicity, and in the same author's dramatization of *Jane Eyre* we do not see Lowood Institution; Jane relates something of her unhappy schooldays to Mr. Rochester when these experiences are already behind her.

Nowadays much more stress is laid on the duty of a playwright who takes a theme from history to be historically accurate; Shakespeare and his contemporaries could happily

Conventions

rely on one book or even on oral traditions; the modern dramatist is expected to do some reading in such places as the British Museum, and any serious distortion or anachronism will bring a flood of angry letters. The special type of historical play or film known as a *documentary* carries this to its extreme with long quotations from actual sources. Yet the dramatist writing a historical play is still under the old obligation to select episodes that are dramatically interesting and to link them convincingly, unless the play is frankly a chronicle rather than a drama.

Nowadays *Othello* would have to be billed as 'Othello— a tragedy . . . adapted from the story by Giraldi Cinthio . . . by William Shakespeare'. This would be a less truthful title spiritually than the present one, since Shakespeare's is by far the greater work. The study of the 'source' of a Shakespeare play can seem very dull; it may appear to involve merely the memorization of a long string of names that have tiresome differences in each version, and a summary of a story that has the same kind of annoyingly trivial difficulties that are difficult to keep clear in the head. Yet, again, if we think of the difference between drama and prose literature and treat our script as an intended performance we shall find the study of sources interesting and illuminating. Why did Shakespeare choose this story? and why did he choose to alter it or alter the proportions of emphasis in such a manner? The answer can usually be found in the practical needs of the theatre; and if we can give a reason for a change we can generally remember it more easily.

Let us take in detail, as an example, *Othello* and its source. As I have implied above, the story of the play is taken from an Italian tale. It is found in the *Hecatommithi* of Giambattista Giraldi, best known as Giraldi Cinthio (1504–1573), who was nearly contemporary with Shakespeare and was himself a playwright, a fact which may help to account for the dramatic possibilities to be seen in his stories, just as today the novels of Somerset Maugham lend themselves very well to dramatization. So far as we know

Adaptation of Plots

Shakespeare did not have access to an English version of this; he may have read it in French, Spanish or the original Italian. (Shakespeare's precise linguistic attainments are not known.) The tale by Cinthio is set in Cyprus and includes the name Desdemona; Shakespeare seems to have selected the rest of the proper names himself from other books. The story is an unmistakable source with very close resemblances not only in plot but also in character-types; but there are important differences which will now be discussed to show how a good story is adapted for dramatic purposes.

First, the Moor and his beloved wife arrived at Cyprus with a calm sea, whereas in the play there is a dangerous storm, described in notably beautiful language. Greater stress is laid in Cinthio's tale on the unlawful love of the wicked Iago[1] for the Moor's wife and one of the motives for wrecking the marriage is this passion—a motive Shakespeare touches on in a couple of lines but does not treat as important. When Iago steals the handkerchief, he does so not by means of his wife, but by taking it himself from Desdemona's girdle when she is playing affectionately with his own little daughter. Cassio[1] knows that the handkerchief is Desdemona's and makes an unsuccessful attempt to return it to her, whereas in the play he does not recognize it. Not only is the Moor, in the tale, deceived by seeing Cassio and Iago in conversation about what he supposes to be a love affair with his wife, but he later sees Cassio's wife copying the design on the handkerchief. Cassio in the play is provided not with a wife but with a lady friend of dubious reputation. The murder as told by Cinthio is less tragic but uglier: Desdemona is beaten to death, with Iago striking the first blow, and part of the house is then pulled down on top of her to make her death look like an accident. The end of the story moves more slowly than the end of the play, being spread over a longer period. The Moor becomes almost mad with grief, turns against Iago and degrades him from his

[1] These names are not in Cinthio, but it makes for clarity and conciseness to use them here.

69

rank. Iago, desiring revenge, reveals the murder and the Moor is taken to Venice and tortured to obtain a confession. He does not confess and is thus not executed, but banished; tardy justice catches up with him when he is killed by the relatives of Desdemona. Iago dies, not as the penalty for the part he had played in the murder of Desdemona, but as a result of tortures inflicted upon him in connection with other crimes. His wife survives to tell the story. With these exceptions the plot of *Othello* is very like the Italian tale.

It is easier to remember these differences if we take them one by one and see how they fit the needs of drama. First, Shakespeare introduces the tempest as the Moor and his wife are coming from Cyprus. Why is this more dramatically effective than a voyage on a calm sea? In real life a rough crossing often has such very unromantic associations as wet clothes and sea-sickness, but in the play it gives opportunities for suspense; we see the Cypriots and some of Othello's staff waiting for the two separate ships in which husband and wife are to arrive. Why on earth should a newly-married pair, passionately in love, travel in separate vessels? They arrive within a few minutes of one another, so it cannot be argued that Othello has administrative preparations or Desdemona domestic preparations to make; the dramatic purpose of the storm and the separate arrivals is threefold; it gives the suspense already mentioned; it gives an opportunity to show, in eloquent greetings, the passionate love of the couple; and it not only gives the opportunity for two very beautiful entrances, but provides one of the finest strokes of irony in all Shakespeare, when at the ecstatic reunion Othello says:

> It gives me wonder great as my conetent
> To see you here before me. O my soul's joy!
> If after every tempest come such calms,
> May the winds blow till they have waken'd death!
> And let the labouring bark climb hills of seas
> Olympus-high and duck again as low

As hell's from heaven! If it were now to die,
'Twere now to be most happy; for I fear,
My soul hath her content so absolute
That not another comfort like to this
Succeeds in unknown fate.

Act II, Sc. 1

Why does Shakespeare not stress the idea of Iago's hatred
for Desdemona originating, as hatred sometimes does, in an
unrequited, unlawful passion? Because, in *Othello*, it is,
from the beginning, Iago's hatred of Othello that is important. Iago does not hate Desdemona; he is more or less indifferent to her, although he says in one particularly cynical
speech that he loves her; part of the ugliness of his character
is precisely this passionless capacity to use an innocent person as an instrument, and I think much of the horror of Iago
is that he feels nothing as human and excusable as a misplaced passion or a resentful jealousy; his obsessive, merci-
less hatred of Othello has as its direct cause the promotion of
Cassio over him. The theme of misplaced love for Desdemona is not, however, wasted, for it can be used to emphasize Desdemona's lovability; it is transferred to a new
character, the weak and stupid Roderigo, whom Iago
despises and uses as a source of money. Roderigo is a weak,
foolish young puppy; but he is human in his weaknesses and
we are made to feel that under some good influence he might
have led quite a good life; Shakespeare deliberately shows a
difference between ordinary human weakness and diabolical
wickedness. Thus the modifications of the plot contribute
to the power of the characterization.

It might be said that the stealing of the handkerchief
would be more dramatic in Cinthio's version; the vileness
of Iago is certainly emphasized by the picture of a man continuing a cruel plot in the presence of his little daughter, who
of all creatures in the world might be expected to soften him;
Shakespeare certainly knew the dramatic effectiveness of the
innocent prattle of young children, as in Macduff's young

71

son or Prince Arthur, but he has already suggested the almost impersonal evil of Iago, and to give him a child would make him seem too normal and human; then, in Shakespeare's play, the wife of Iago is given a more interesting part by being the person who steals the handkerchief. But there is more subtlety than this in the alteration. In Cinthio's story Desdemona loses her handkerchief through kindness to a child; in Shakespeare she loses it actually through kindness to her own husband, for she drops it after trying to bind his aching head. This adds to the pathos of her downfall. Again, if Emilia had had a child she might have been less ready to die for her mistress.

The substitution of a somewhat disreputable lady friend for Cassio's wife is an economy of persons—in the tale Cassio has both!—and has the further effect both of making Iago's accusation at least more possible and of making the gift by Cassio of the handkerchief to the woman seem more insulting to Desdemona.

The different circumstances of the death of Desdemona are obviously dictated partly by sheer necessity of staging. Even on the modern stage it would not be easy to represent part of the house being pulled down over the body of Desdemona; on the Elizabethan stage it would have been impossible. The boy who then played Desdemona might have found the process of battering to death each night too exhausting—a pretended smothering in the bedclothes is safer and less painful, and makes it easier for the 'corpse' to lie still for the longish period after the 'death'. But there are motives more truly artistic than these practical necessities. It is much more tragic if the loving husband kills his wife unaided; the terrible intimacy of the last interview would be absent if Iago were in the room, and the Iago of Shakespeare is far too clever to have an actual hand in the murder. In Shakespeare's Othello's tortured mind the death of Desdemona is seen as a holy obligation, a kind of sacrifice of what is most loved, an impulse appropriate to him as still half a barbarian, and he can thus be shown as essentially good in all his near-madness and reluctant cruelty. The play would not be a true tragedy if we did not feel sympathy for Othello, if we were not conscious of him as a good man in error.

It should hardly be necessary to show the greater suitability to drama of the Shakespearian ending of the story. In order to bring about the dénouement rapidly it is necessary for Othello to learn that he was mistaken; thus we have the sacrifice of Emilio, a moving episode, extremely effective on the stage and underlining the theme of sacrifice. (In productions the bed is often made to resemble an altar.) Iago's wickedness, too, can now be further emphasized; he now kills his wife, but not in any anguish of conflict and tenderness, merely in an ugly temper because she has endangered him. This makes the crime of Othello more forgivable by contrast. Then, Othello at the end is not merely a murderer brought to justice, as in Cinthio's Sunday-paper tale; he is allowed to show his sense of honour, explaining himself with dignity and choosing immediate death rather than the disgrace of a trial, and his overwhelming remorse, proving at the last that he loved his wife in his inadequate way. This is less horrible than the prose tale, but more truly tragic, for tragedy is of the mind rather than the body. Iago is condemned at once to be tortured to death for his crime, and this satisfies the audience, who wish to see justice done here, though we do not usually feel vindictive to any of Shakespeare's characters. The delayed justice of the tale might be very effective in a novel and might bear more resemblance to real life, but the story of the play has great concentration and the close sequence of events required for great drama.

It would be a good exercise for the student of drama to take the source of some other Shakespeare play and make this kind of detailed comparison, trying to account for all the changes. Shakespeare usually creates the individual characters almost completely. The exercise is made easy by the fact that any annotated text of Shakespeare will contain something on 'sources'. (For this purpose the 'Arden' edition is perhaps the best, though it is expensive.) It is also very interesting to take an old play that Shakespeare used as a source, such as *The Troublesome Raigne of King John*, *Leir*, and *Promos and Cassandra*[1] and see how Shakespeare transformed these very ordinary plays into works of genius.

Another useful and exciting exercise is to take two plays on the same theme and compare the treatments of the theme. This is limited by the number of such plays available, but includes: *The Choephoroe* of Aeschylus with the *Electra* of Euripides and perhaps with Eugene O'Neill's *Mourning Becomes Electra*; the *Hippolytus* of Euripides with the *Phèdre* of Racine; the *Iphigenia* of Euripides with the versions by Racine and Goethe; Marlowe's *Dr. Faustus* with Goethe's *Faust*. T. S. Eliot has also said that his *The Cocktail Party* is a version of the *Alcestis* of Euripides, though here the equivalence is much less obvious. There are also operatic versions of several works of fiction, such as Donizetti's *Lucia di Lammermoor* (based on Sir Walter Scott's *The Bride of Lammermoor*), Bizet's *Carmen* (based on Prosper Merimée's story), Benjamin Britten's *Peter Grimes* (based on a verse tale by Crabbe) and Arthur Benjamin's setting of *A Tale of Two Cities*. Musical as well as dramatic considerations are, of course, important here.

[1] Perhaps the source of *Measure for Measure*. The story is also found in Cinthio.

V. THE CONVENTIONAL
DIVISIONS

This is my play's last scene.
JOHN DONNE: *Holy Sonnets*

THIS is intended as an elementary book, but it may perhaps seem insultingly elementary to say anything
about acts and scenes. Every schoolboy who wants to
concoct a thrilling drama of atom-bomb espionage, every
schoolgirl with an idea for a play about Bonnie Prince
Charlie, knows enough to head the second page of an
exercise book, 'ACT I, SCENE I'. Yet it is not really so simple,
so it may be useful to say a few words about act and scene
divisions.

There are, of course, plays with no act or scene division.
The most obvious example is the form of play, now extremely popular with amateurs and including many good
plays, known as the *one-act play*. This, in its pure form, is a
play lasting about 25 to 45 minutes; the action is thus very
concentrated. Much rubbish in this genre exists, but it also
includes such miniature masterpieces as J. M. Synge's *Riders
to the Sea*, Sean O'Casey's *A Pound on Demand*, Lady
Gregory's *The Rising of the Moon*, Shaw's *The Dark Lady of
the Sonnets* and Christopher Fry's *A Phoenix Too Frequent*.
There are some longer plays which go on without a break,
but are not the usual kind of one-act play; examples are the
anonymous *Everyman* and Terence Rattigan's *The Browning
Version*. This type of play generally concentrates on a single
critical occasion, tragic or comic, in the lives of several
people, and leads to one major climax and dénouement.
Pageants, films and radio plays are generally performed

75

without act or scene divisions, though we can often perceive divisions of a less formal kind.

The Greek drama has no act or scene divisions in the sense in which the modern drama uses them; the action is uninterrupted; but division of the action is made by the Chorus reciting lyrics or invocations to the gods between the episodes. The same is true of plays closely modelled on the Greek, such as Milton's *Samson Agonistes* and T. S. Eliot's *Murder in the Cathedral*. This kind of division is obviously suitable only for poetic drama.

The French practice, bewildering to English eyes, is to assume in printed scripts that a new scene begins whenever a new person enters or leaves:

Scene V. ANDROMAQUE, CÉPHISE

ANDROMAQUE

Quel mépris la cruelle attache à ses refus!

CÉPHISE

Je croirois ses conseils, et je verrois Pyrrhus.
Un regard confondroit Hermione et la Grèce . . .
Mais lui-même il vous cherche.

Scene VI. PYRRHUS, ANDROMAQUE, PHOENIX, CÉPHISE

PYRRHUS à PHOENIX

Où donc est la princesse?
Ne m'avois-tu pas dit qu'elle étoile en ces lieux?

JEAN RACINE: *Andromaque*

Some Restoration comedies, such as Congreve's *The Way of the World*, were also printed in this way. In a French script 'scene' thus refers simply to a movement on the stage; 'act' indicates a change of setting or a lapse of time. In English practice either 'act' or 'scene' denotes one or both of these alterations, and, since the introduction of curtains, the lowering and raising of the curtain. In the British theatre the 'act' is normally one of the chief divisions of the play, the 'scene' a subdivision of an act.

The development of the use of realistic scenery and curtains has made a great difference to the significance of act and scene divisions. When there was no scenery to be shifted a play could include as many different imaginary scenes as the writer liked. Shakespeare's *Antony and Cleopatra* has forty-two scenes, some of only a few lines, according to the modern editions, which may not always be divided exactly as Shakespeare intended. *Macbeth*, in which the setting is much more restricted, and the action more concentrated, has twenty-eight. Productions of Shakespeare on the stage of today have had to solve the problems presented by these frequent changes of scene by cutting out some short and unimportant scenes; by reviving Elizabethan methods of production; by the use of a revolving stage or a set that can be darkened quickly in one section or a special adjustment of complicated curtaining; by playing scenes in front of the curtain or on different parts of the stage. A play written for the modern stage never demands so many shifts of scene. It is now customary, though not a rigid rule, for a full-length modern play to have three acts, and very often each act contains only one scene. But there are successful modern plays with only two acts or as many as five, and some plays still have one act or more, subdivided into scenes. Not only are Sheridan's *The Rivals* and *The School for Scandal* five-act plays; so is Flecker's *Hassan* (1922), and there are other enormous exceptions to the three-act pattern, such as Shaw's *Man and Superman* and *Back to Methusaleh*—both too long to be played, usually, in their entirety. *The Dog Beneath the Skin* has fourteen scenes and choruses, but the authors call it 'a play in three acts'. Radio drama can have many more scenes than visible drama, but only in the sense that a division can be indicated by a few bars of music or a sound effect. Where a three-act non-experimental play has further division into scenes, it is generally because a change of scene is quite unavoidable, or the curtain falls and rises to indicate a short lapse of time, as in R. E. Sherwood's *Idiot's Delight*.

Acts and scenes are, in a way, merely formal divisions of no great artistic importance; they allow the scene to be changed when necessary; they allow the cast a few moments of rest or time to change a costume; and, in the modern commercial theatre, they give members of the audience a chance to go and have a whisky and soda or powder hot noses. Incidentally a Shakespeare play, though always a five-acter, is nowadays generally produced with the normal two intervals; if this making of it into a three-acter seems a little barbarous, we should bear in mind that the texts of the time were very careless about act and scene division.

Act and scene divisions are not nearly as essential to drama as plot; in a well-made play they closely follow the requirements of the plot. What is is interesting and worth our attention is how the dramatist makes use of act and scene divisions technically. This is mostly a recent development. In Shakespeare's plays a rhyming couplet was very often used to indicate the end of a scene. It could be dignified:

Edmund: As for the mercy
      Which he intends to Lear, and to Cordelia,
      The battle done, and they within our power,
      Shall never see his pardon; for my state
      Stands on me to defend, not to debate. (*Exit*)
                    King Lear, Act V, Sc. 1

or it could be almost comically banal and artificial:

    We came into the world like brother and brother;
    And now let's go hand in hand, not one before the other.
            The Comedy of Errors, Act V, Sc. 1

The same device is used in other plays of the period:

    Stars fall but in the grossness of our sight,
    A good man dying, th'earth doth lose a light.
      JOHN FORD: *The Broken Heart*, Act II, Sc. 3

These end-of-scene couplets gave the dramatist the opportunity to throw in some general observation in the manner of a proverb, or, when it was well done as in the first example, to end the scene crisply with a definite feeling of conclusiveness.

Nowadays the 'exit lines' of actors and the 'curtain line' at the end of a scene are regarded as very important to the artistic structure of the play; this is a comparatively recent development. This is to carry over the suspense and excitement to the next act or scene, and, in the case of the 'exit line', to give the actor the chance to make a strong impression before going out. An example of the very strong curtain will be found in Charlotte Hastings's play *Bonaventure*, a murder mystery with a good deal of real characterization and moral interest. As a result of a flood, some strangers shelter in a convent hospital. We see the gentle, orderly atmosphere and some of the spiritual difficulties of Sister Mary Bonaventure; and in the last few lines of the first act we suddenly learn that the woman who has been brought in is a woman condemned to death for murder and attended by a male and a female guard. This leaves any normally inquisitive person with a strong desire to see what happens next. A key revelation may be made in the last line of a scene; or a curtain line may be specially chosen because it is one of the best jokes in a comedy. The exit lines of the characters in Emlyn Williams's *The Corn is Green* are well worth studying to show how they strengthen the impression a character has made. This special skill was not much used by the earlier dramatists and, where it was used, may not have been conscious; but it could be argued that some modern dramatists were a little too self-conscious in underlining all their act and scene divisions and gave an impression, especially in light comedy, of over-artificiality. It is for the student to decide.

VI. DIRECT EXPERIENCE OF CHARACTERS

> For nature hath with sovereyn diligence
> Y-formed hir in so greet excellence,
> As though she wolde seyn, 'lo! I, Nature,
> Thus can I forme and peynte a creature,
> When that me list; who can me countrefete?'
>
> CHAUCER: *The Phisiciens Tale*

WE must not forget that drama is not life, though it is the most literal imitation of life to be found in the arts of the writer. Those who most insist that painting should be representational, like photography, seldom realize that in fact even such 'representational' pictures as those of Vermeer or Hals are strikingly different from photographs; it is probably true to say that all so-called artistic 'imitation' is really in part a heightening; but this is especially so in the drama with its recognized conventions.

The concentration of a play makes it necessary for the portrayal of character to be very rapid. It must also, usually, be clear and unambiguous, though some of the most fascinating dramatic characters are open to more than one interpretation; Hamlet and Cleopatra, Creon in *Antigone*, King Oedipus, and, on a lower level, Blanche Dubois in *A Streetcar Named Desire*, or even the King of Siam in *The King and I*, are examples of this; but if most dramatic characters were not simple these complex characters would not stand out as unusual and worthy of special discussion. In real life we do seek to 'get to know' a person we like, and fully expect it to take a long time; most of us wear a number of self-protective masks over our real personalities; we soon find out that it is never possible to know a person fully even when we have lived with them for years. Indeed, we cannot really claim to know ourselves. In real life the knowledge of people's characters is hampered by such factors as: the reticence of modesty, the feeling that *my* life is of no interest to anyone else; the reticence of cowardice, arising out of a sense of our own vulnerability if we are really known; the reticence of social usage, which puts a more or less strict taboo on the divulging of our economic position, emotional life and family relationships, though, oddly enough, it lays no such taboo on the less interesting and often disagreeable discussion of illness, provided that the illness affects a mentionable part of the human anatomy; and the difficulty, when, as between people deeply in love or trusting friends, most of the barriers are broken down, of finding words to express the most interesting things about ourselves or our relationships anyway. We seldom, in real life, learn as much in two hours about a person as we do about Lady Macbeth, Othello, Rosalind or Euripides' Medea. Persons in plays are amazingly communicative.

If we find someone interesting we can usually arrange to meet them again, or, failing that, to write to them; in a play we must be told at one sitting all the details of a personality that are of interest. (In a re-reading of the script we may notice some details that escaped us at first, and when we study a part for acting we may find many subtleties that we should otherwise have missed; but all these things were there to be seen from the beginning and our obtuseness is at fault.) The dramatist, with this task of unnaturally rapid communication, thus resorts, in those plays in which character is of importance, to one or more of the following accepted conventions which allow a greater revelation than in real life.

Especially in the earlier drama, an interesting character may explain himself more or less directly to the audience in a soliloquy ('alone-speech'). The soliloquy in a play is intended to be a direct and sincere expression of the speaker's real thoughts, with the conventional not true to life, triple

assumption, that we know ourselves, that we think in gram-
matically coherent language and that we speak these thoughts
aloud. Brutus in *Julius Caesar* is shown as a man sensitive,
loyal, kindly, honest, if anything too puritanical and scrupu-
lous about moral obligations, to the extent of demanding
more than is human from others and from himself. Yet this
man is to be shown also as assassinating a statesman who
was not grossly tyrannical, not vicious, and who had been
his good friend—an act of rare and ugly ingratitude. To
make this a tolerable psychological possibility, Shakespeare
must show Brutus in a state of mental conflict:

Brutus: It must be by his death: and, for my part,
         I know no personal cause to spurn at him,
         But for the general. He would be crown'd:—
         How that might change his nature, there's the ques-
           tion:
         It is the bright day that brings forth the adder;
         And that craves wary walking. Crown him?—
           that;—
         And then, I grant, we put a sting in him,
         That at his will he may do danger with.
         The abuse of greatness is, when it disjoins
         Remorse from power: and, to speak truth of Caesar,
         I have not known when his affections swayed
         More than his reason. But 'tis a common proof,
         That lowliness is young ambition's ladder,
         Whereto the climber-upward turns his face;
         But when he once attains the topmost round,
         He then unto the ladder turns his back,
         Looks in the clouds, scorning the base degrees
         By which he did ascend: so Caesar may;
         Then, lest he may prevent. And since the quarrel
         Will bear no colour for the thing he is,
         Fashion it thus; that what he is, augmented,
         Would run to these and these extremities:
         And therefore think him as a serpent's egg,

Which, hatcht, would, as his kind, grow mischiev-
ous;
And kill him in the shell.

Act II, Sc. 1.

We are given this soliloquy and several other speeches,
which, if they do not convince us that Brutus is right in killing his friend, show us how Brutus, by his very loftiness of
character, could have succeeded in convincing himself that
he was right. The soliloquies of Hamlet and Macbeth in
states of mental conflict are even better known.

Another valuable use of the soliloquy is to reveal a hypocrite. A hypocrite is one of the most difficult characters to
portray on the stage, as opposed to the novel, in which he
can be described as well as speak for himself and a larger
variety of actions can be shown, for if he is a successful
hypocrite he does not discuss his real motives with anyone
and is, indeed, elaborately cautious in concealing them.
When we hear Iago talking to Othello and trying to make
him suspect his innocent wife, we must not be allowed to
feel that no sensible man would be deluded by such a slimy
villain. If Othello were simply stupidly credulous we should
be sorry for Desdemona, but we should not feel the overwhelming tragedy of the wreck of a beautiful marriage and
the agony of a good man. We must be made to feel that Iago
is horribly plausible, that he is successful in giving the impression of being an honest, blunt but sympathetic friend
with a great deal of worldly experience, reluctantly mention-
ing painful facts. We do receive this impression. However,
if Iago seemed honest all the time we might ourselves be
deluded and believe that the tragedy was all a sad mistake
with no villain. So we hear a soliloquy which leaves us in no
doubt of Iago's bad intentions and callousness:

> Thus do I ever make my fool my purse;
> For I my own gain'd knowledge would profane
> If I would time expend with such a snipe,
> But for my sport and profit. I hate the Moor;

Conventions

And it is thought abroad, that 'twixt my sheets
'has done my office: I know not if 't be true:
But I, for mere suspicion in that kind,
Will do it as for surety. He holds me well;
The better shall my purpose work upon him.
Cassio's a proper man: let me see now;
To get his place, and to plume up my will
In double knavery—How, how?—let's see:—
After some time, to abuse Othello's ear
That he is too familiar with his wife:—
He hath a person, and a smooth dispose,
To be suspected; framed to make women false.
The Moor is of a free and open nature,
That thinks men honest that but seem to be so;
And will as tenderly be led by the nose
As asses are.
I have't; it is engender'd:—hell and night
Must bring this monstrous birth to the world's light.

Othello, Act I, Sc. 3

Now, in real life, an Iago would probably not be nearly as honest with himself about his motives; he would probably not even be aware of them; far more wrong is done by people who think they are doing right, from some honest mistake or that self-deception which we all practise more or less, than by the rare people who wilfully choose to do what is wrong. On the stage we accept such soliloquies as a means of showing what is going on in a character's mind. In fact most of us do not analyze our motives and plan our actions as rationally and consciously as do Shakespearian soliloquizers; and anything we think in words is the barest diagram of the four-dimensional chaos of feelings, memories, needs, secret wishes, images, dreams and associations that occupies the normal human mind.

Attempts to demonstrate something of the real complexity and irrationality of the human mind have been made in a few modern plays such as Tyrone Guthrie's *Top of the Ladder* in which soliloquies have a dream-like, almost surrealist quality and memories are dramatized as a man is dying; Anne Ridler's *The Mask* and *The Missing Bridegroom*, plays about the deeper problems of personality; and parts of T. S. Eliot's *The Family Reunion*. (It will be noticed that all these plays are more or less poetic.) Eugene O'Neill's enormously long play *Strange Interlude* seeks to show the complexity of real human motives by the use of soliloquies and asides.

However, the soliloquy is a relatively primitive form of dramatic expression and is not generally accepted as a dramatic device today without some further trick to soften its artificiality. In a stage performance of *Hamlet* the soliloquies can still be spoken; but in the splendid film, using a modern medium and appealing to an audience many of whom were not experienced theatre-goers, Sir Laurence Olivier had to make it clear that the soliloquies represented the speaker's thoughts. The same device of letting the face remain motionless while the words ran off the sound-track was used in the film of *Henry V*. Nowadays soliloquy is usually acceptable only in very unusual circumstances such as the portrayal of madness, or in highly experimental drama such as the speeches of Tom in Tennessee Williams's 'memory play' of neurotics, *The Glass Menagerie* and some of the long speeches in Louis MacNeice's *Out of the Picture*; softened by such a device as making the speaker address an animal, a picture or some other object, for example Alan with the Dog in Auden and Isherwood's *The Dog Beneath the Skin*; or where the dramatist achieves a comic effect by admitting that the whole thing is a pretence and a character can therefore approach the front of the stage and talk directly to the audience, as in Sacha Guitry's *Don't Listen, Ladies!*

Another conventional method of conveying information about events or character has been, and still is, the use of the *confidant(e)*.[1] This is a character in whom a more important person of the play can confide, and is almost always a

---

[1] Modern usage distinguishes the male and female; early usage was less particular.

Conventions

trusted friend of the same sex. Horatio in *Hamlet*, Celia in
As You Like It, the Nurse in *Romeo and Juliet*, Nerissa in
The Merchant of Venice, Mosca in Jonson's *Volpone*, Ventidius in Dryden's *All for Love*, Miss Susan in Barrie's *Quality Street*, are examples of this, though in these as in all good plays a confidant(e) has also personality and a real part in the action. Obviously, this device can be overworked or mishandled by a clumsy dramatist. However, used with reasonable verisimilitude the device is very useful, and is more acceptable to the modern playgoer than the soliloquy, for people do not usually talk much to themselves except in such unrevealing mutterings as, 'Put potatoes in . . . turn oven down . . . grate cheese . . . drat, that's my finger . . .' but most of us do sometimes feel the need to talk over our personal problems with some trusted friend, and do, in suitable company, have spells of unaccustomed frankness. As in real life, so in a play, we can generally assume that what an important character says to a selected person like this is at least what he or she believes to be the truth, while there may be reticence or hypocrisy in talking to other people.

We also learn about characters in plays, as in life, by their actions, and a comparatively trivial action may have great significance in preparing us for a character before that character is confronted with a grave decision. Hamlet comes into a heartlessly gay, somewhat corrupt court wearing a black cloak; from this alone, without his speaking a word, we know that he alone is still mourning for his father, that he feels unhappy and a misfit and that he has the moral courage to show his feelings. Cleopatra shows her violent temper in a scene in which she personally beats a bringer of bad news; but we have had a hint of it earlier in her none too regal threat to her maid:

> By Isis, I will give thee bloody teeth,
> If thou with Caesar paragon again
> My man of men.
>
> *Antony and Cleopatra*, Act I, Sc. 5

Direct Experience of Characters

The essential goodness and gentleness of Brutus is indicated by his gracious treatment of the boy Lucius. The wicked Queen in *Cymbeline* not only plans the death of an innocent and noble girl, but shows her callousness by making cruel experiments on animals her untruthful justification for wanting poisons. In Jonson's *The Silent Woman*, Morose, who can bear no noise, devises innumerable small rules and contrivances to avoid being troubled with noise, and every one of these details adds to the general impression. Indeed, if it were not for the details that prove Morose is unreasonable and childishly self-centred in his pursuit of quiet, we might be tempted to be sorry for him and find the comedy a near-tragedy, for the central plot, in which he believes himself to be married to a noisy, scolding woman of scandalous reputation, is a situation in which the most reasonable of men might be distressed. At the beginning of James Bridie's *Daphne Laureola*, the modesty and idealism of the young Pole Ernest Piaste is shown, before he begins to play an important part in the action, by his quiet and civil manner in a restaurant where a number of other people are giggling, talking loudly, trying to make black-market deals, arguing and blustering in various unpleasant ways. As, a little later, he is to hit someone on the head from rather misplaced chivalry, it is important that we should first be convinced of his natural good manners!

As in life, we often learn about characters in a play from what other people say about them, and, as in life, we do not always have to believe all that other people say. A startlingly extreme example of this is J. B. Priestley's *Dangerous Corner*, in which practically the villain of the piece is a man called Martin, who died before the play begins and whom we never see. We never see him in the flesh, no; but the discussion of his character, motives and actions by other people, who were all closely bound to him by love, hatred or circumstances, creates the whole plot of the play. In Shakespeare a character is quite often introduced by a speech from someone shrewd and trustworthy who

87

Conventions

gives us a clue to the impression we may expect to receive:

Helena: . . . Who comes here?
One that goes with him; I love him for his sake;
And yet I know him a notorious liar,
Think him a great way fool, solely a coward;
Yet these fix'd evils sit so fit in him,
That they take place, when virtue's steely bones
Look bleak in the cold wind: withal, full oft we see
Cold wisdom waiting on superfluous folly.
                    All's Well that Ends Well, Act I, Sc. 1

These lines are spoken just before the first entry of Parolles. In Shaw, too, there are such spoken preparations, as in the very illuminating discussion of Saint Joan before she appears. We may also think of Hamlet's brief savage introduction of the 'chough' Osric; the first speech of *Antony and Cleopatra*, a bitter comment by a Roman soldier on the infatuation we are about to see; the discussion of Benedick before he appears in *Much Ado About Nothing*, which fulfils the double function of telling us something about Benedick and showing us something of Beatrice, while hinting that she is not uninterested in him. There are many possible modifications of this technique.

It is possible for the playwright to keep the audience guessing, instead of giving enlightenment; for instance, in Synge's *The Playboy of the Western World* much is said about Christy Mahon's father long before he appears, and a good deal of the comedy arises out of the fact that some of what is said is true, some not. In *Measure for Measure*, in which the central theme is a puritanical man's discovery that he is not as irreproachable as he had believed himself to be, and his exposure, the Duke and Lucio both speak at some length of Angelo's chastity in dignified language and after we have learned that he is really not very virtuous, Lucio continues to speak in more flippant language of his famous coldness, so that the reputation he has built up is emphasized and the

88

difference between reputation and character made more forceful. In J. B. Priestley's *Bright Shadow*, a detective drama, the chief interest lies in the unravelling of actions and character, the gradual reaching the truth by clearing up various misconceptions of the early part of the play. A truly great drama whose interest is partly of this kind is Ibsen's *The Wild Duck*.

The dramatist, in letting people talk about each other, can sometimes throw dust in our eyes; it is not always easy to be sure whether this is being done deliberately or not. In Strindberg's terrible play *The Dance of Death* we are told, right at the end of the play, that an apparently singularly unlovable though very unhappy character 'was a good man', with great emphasis, and we are left to interpret this as we please. In many of the plays of Shakespeare characters of very dubious worth are gilded by being associated with very beautiful language, either in their own speeches or in the things other people say about them: Bassanio and Jessica in *The Merchant of Venice*, Posthumus Leonatus in *Cymbeline*, Claudio in *Much Ado About Nothing*, Florizel in *The Winter's Tale* and to some extent Bertram in *All's Well That Ends Well*—though even Helena's admiration cannot glorify the last for long. Shakespeare has a gift for dazzling us with leaping fountains of wonderful language, and it is sometimes necessary to discern whether the beautiful language is there just because Shakespeare could not help writing well or because it is appropriate to the speaker or subject. It may be intended to improve the impression made by a character who is intended to be sympathetic but has faults that might alienate the audience; it may be employed from, or concerning, a character because their appeal lies mostly in their eloquence or lyrical setting—equally true, perhaps, of Falstaff and Perdita—or it may sometimes be marvellously appropriate to the depth and beauty of a character, as in the imaginative richness of Othello's language or the pathetic sweetness of Ophelia's.

Needless to say, most people do not stop talking about

a character after that character has appeared; we learn much from what people say *to* another person, or about that person in subsequent comment or explanation. This is going on almost continuously in those plays in which character is important, for good plays are mostly conversation.

In drama, people are usually much more frank about themselves and less liable to self-deception than most of us are in real life; but we must bear in mind, in all descriptions of a character by other persons in the play, not only the character being described but the nature of the person who is speaking. For instance, Cleopatra despises Octavia; this does not mean that Octavia is to be despised, for Cleopatra is a woman of jealous temperament and Octavia is her rival; it takes either a very cold or a very magnanimous woman to be fair to a rival in love, and catty underrating through jealousy is not confined to one sex. Iago thinks Othello a fool; but Othello's employers respect him, and Iago is the kind of man who thinks anything great-hearted is folly because it is outside his comprehension. In Shakespeare as in life people in the first flush of young love frequently overestimate the people they love, and other people underestimate their rivals or enemies, or people who commit only the crime of being different from them. Sir Toby Belch presumes to despise Malvolio, who is an unlikeable character, being a puritan, a pompous egotist and a prig, but Malvolio is doing a responsible task properly, which is more than Sir Toby is doing; on the other hand, it is Malvolio's complete inability to see a joke, in a houseful of frivolous people, that undoes him. We must always remember, when studying an opinion on someone given in a play, whether the speaker is an enemy, a friend or indifferent; whether he or she is intelligent, stupid, ignorant, educated, especially narrowminded or especially endowed with sympathetic insight; we must also remember to whom the opinion is expressed, what motive other than truthfulness may lie behind that expression and whether the speech is appropriate to the speaker or put in by the dramatist to give an explanation that cannot be postponed. Sometimes a very minor character is given great insight; an enemy may speak more fairly than would be likely in real life, or a servant be more communicative.

We should remember, too, that a dramatist does not portray exclusively characters of whom he approves, and the test of his skill in characterization is whether he can show us many different kinds of people and make them all equally convincing while they are on the stage. One occasionally encounters a stupid objection to a novel or play on the ground that it contains unpleasant characters; if the drama is to bear any resemblance to life it must contain both good and bad people, with some good in the bad characters and some bad in the good; a play containing angels exclusively, devils exclusively or even angels and devils in black and white uniforms is to that extent an unconvincing play, though if the action is exciting it may still be a success, at least commercially.

Shakespeare's greatness does not lie in plot or originality; his plots are generally borrowed, often ill-constructed; and he has no really original ideas; but as a creator of characters who seem to live like real human beings, provoke discussion, and linger in our memories, he has no rival. We have only to contrast a late play by Shakespeare with one of the best plays of Ben Jonson—a much more careful craftsman and probably a more learned man—to see the difference between breathing characters and very well handled, but at last unsatisfying types. It is useful to learn to distinguish types, who are often traditional figures and can be summarized in a few words: the morbidly jealous husband, the go-between, the boastful coward, the nagging wife, the spendthrift son, the charming and unsophisticated young girl, the lover, the severe parent, the helpful adviser, the pompous official, the comic servant. Some of the stock types are as old as the classical comedy, which had special masks and wigs for them; we have also developed new stage types such as the negro, the Scotsman, the Irishman, the Jew—but there are also profound and tragic stage Jews, especially since the Euro-

Conventions

pean experience of Fascism—the schoolteacher and the Civil Servant, who are often grossly over-simplified and distorted.

Some quite interesting and meritorious plays contain only types; but the greatest plays contain some more rounded and complex characters. Ford in *The Merry Wives of Windsor* is little more than a stock 'jealous husband', like Kitely in Jonson's *Every Man in his Humour*; Othello, Antony and Leontes are very much more. Hero in *Much Ado About Nothing* and perhaps even Ophelia in *Hamlet* are little more than touching figures of injured innocence; we almost expect each of them to be turned out into a snowstorm; but Imogen in *Cymbeline* has a great deal of character in every sense of the word and is one of the strongest and noblest female characters Shakespeare ever drew. It is a pity that she is concealed in a play so badly constructed that it is seldom performed.

It is as well, before leaving this topic, to say that in most plays there are major characters and minor characters. In the best plays there is seldom just a hero, a heroine and a villain with some unimportant characters swarming around; there may be six or even ten important figures with life and personality; but it is rare to see a play in which every character has been conceived, as it were, in the round. At first sight the flatness of some of the minor characters may seem like a fault; but in good drama it is another manifestation of that essential of all great art and especially great drama, selection. A play by Shakespeare may well have twenty characters; *Hamlet* has twenty-three, not counting the servants, messengers, lords, ladies, courtiers and attendants necessary for a proper performance. We could not absorb a play in which there were twenty characters of the complexity of Hamlet or even the Queen; moreover, such a play, within the usual time of a performance, would not be possible, for complexity can seldom be revealed in a few lines. On the other hand, Sartre's *Huis Clos* ('*In Camera*') has only three characters, and they can all be given equal importance and great complexity.

Direct Experience of Characters

Shakespeare has a charming gift for making a relatively unimportant figure quite a personality in a small way; so has Shaw. We may think of Dogberry, Fluellen, Launce, Adam, Gratiano, Hubert, Mistress Overdone, and the inimitable Autolycus, who is little more than an ornament in *The Winter's Tale*, but steals the play if the producer is not careful; in Shaw there are Britannicus (*Caesar and Cleopatra*), Mrs. Pearce (*Pygmalion*), Ladvenu (*Saint Joan*) and others. On the whole Marlowe lacked this gift; *Dr. Faustus* is a play of two tremendous personalities, Faustus and Mephistopheles, against a background of cardboard cut-outs; and plenty of fairly successful plays have been written with no profound characterization at all.

Critics often, and understandably, discuss the characters of a great play or novel as if these created personalities were really alive. The most extreme of these imaginative approaches is Mary Cowden Clarke, who in her very readable though now somewhat out-of-date book *The Girlhood of Shakespeare's Heroines* made up a series of intelligent and pleasing stories based on the assumption that from Shakespeare's depiction of his heroines it is possible to deduce a pattern of their childhood and adolescence, much as a skilled psychologist can nowadays do with a real person. Some dramatists have claimed that when they are creating a character that character lives the other part of its life in their minds; they see its imagined childhood and the influences that have shaped it, know what it likes to eat and where it went to school. Other dramatists repudiate this as affected nonsense; the truth is likely to be that different artists work by different methods and that if any method produces great literature it is a good method for that artist. We should, however, keep firmly in mind when studying a script as a work of art—not when seeing the play for the first time in the theatre, when we should surrender as fully as possible to the dramatic illusion—the fact that the characters of a play are not real people. They are the creations of an imagination which, however much more powerful and broad than our

93

Conventions

own, was yet only one man's or woman's mind with personal limitations and prejudices. Strindberg's women are very different from those of Shaw, and Barrie's than those of either, because these dramatists had very different ideas about women and very different experience of them in life; Shakespeare's portrayal of Henry V as a man to be admired is very different from the treatment of power-hungry politicians in Spender's *Trial of a Judge*, Priestley's *Home is Tomorrow* or Auden and Isherwood's *On the Frontier*. We can learn a good deal about an author or about the times in which he lived from his treatment of character, though it is probably true to say that the greater he is the less we shall learn, since genius is generally to be found in company with charity and breadth of mind in proportion to the imaginative and artistic qualities.

We should also remember when studying dramatic characters that we are studying them ourselves with limited minds, which are, in most of us, narrower, less experienced and less imaginative than the mind of a good dramatist. When we say that something is 'untrue to human nature' we may well be right. After all, we do know many human tendencies and probabilities and base all our conduct on some sense of the predictability of human reactions to it. But we must also ask ourselves, whenever we are tempted to say, 'This is not true to human nature', 'Do I mean, untrue to human nature, or merely untrue to human nature in my own extremely limited experience and in my one type of society and one epoch of history?' Euripides makes Medea kill her own children. True, this is an unlikely situation, and a society in which it was taken for granted that mothers might kill their children would be a very unhappy society. But though there are few situations more horrible to the normal mind, such things have been known to happen and are occasionally still reported in the Press; and Euripides makes the crime more probable by making Medea a barbarian, of violent passions, and almost deranged by grief, jealousy and humiliation. Olivia in *Twelfth Night*, a lady of wealth, position, refine-

94

ment and sensitivity, marries a man she hardly knows, in eager haste, and is not distressed when she finds she has accidentally married the brother of the man who first took her fancy and who was a girl in disguise; moreover, the man, a sensible and decent person, is willing immediately to accept a proposal of marriage from a strange lady. Unlikely? Yes; but many wise ladies and gentlemen have done strange things for love, and they have not always regretted it. In this particular play the partners seem reasonably well suited; and it could also be argued that grief for the loss of her brother in Olivia, and the shock and bewilderment of shipwreck and the apparent loss of his twin sister for Sebastian, have made both very hungry for affection and therefore highly susceptible. The answer to people who are too fond of taking upon themselves authority to speak the last word on a subject as wide and as subtle as human nature has been given very wittily and astringently by one critic:

'Life holds far less of the predictable than we find it convenient to assert. And those who would require more "consistency" of Cleopatra are, I would suggest, making the same sort of demand upon a dramatic personage that a society or a culture makes on an individual—the demand that the individual should conform to his definition, that he should, even amid disruptive experiences, indicate the fixity and intelligibility of his character against the fluid and mysterious personality that lies below, that he should do this in the interest of the general lucidity of things.

'For on what sort of common observation, it must be asked, does Schucking rely? Probably few people who venture an opinion on Cleopatra have much acquaintance with dissipated queens, with courtesans or even with harlots. Few have watched a complex woman flee from a sea-battle or reconcile herself with her lover after such a flight or later draw him up, dying, into a beleaguered monument. The number of people who have witnessed a royal suicide must be extremely small.'

J. I. M. STEWART: *Character and Motive in Shakespeare*, 1949

Conventions

However, certainly all we can ourselves learn and observe about human beings helps us in the intelligent appreciation of characterization in the drama. An amazing evidence of Shakespeare's general closeness of observation, imaginative insight and truth to nature is to be found in the fact that some modern psychologists, after researches into the human mind for which Shakespeare had not the equipment, have declared that some of his characters, notably Lear, Hamlet and Ophelia, are accurate clinical examples of how certain mental and nervous disorders develop; and psycho-analytical technique can be used to explain some of these characters. It is even more impressive to show how in the history of Shakesperian criticism his characters have been made to fit, at different times, most of the theories of the human mind that have ever been invented to explain what we still do not fully understand; this is surely a decisive proof that his characters are somehow very like real human beings in spite of the fact that they speak mostly in verse.

VII. THE TECHNIQUE OF
DIALOGUE—INDIVIDUALS

Speed: Item, she doth talk in her sleep.
Launce: It's no matter for that, so she sleep not in her talk.
Speed: Item, she is slow in words.
Launce: O villain, that set this down among her vices! To be slow in
words is a woman's only virtue: I pray thee, out with't, and
place it for her chief virtue.

The Two Gentleman of Verona, Act III, Sc. 1

A PLAY is its dialogue. In a Greek play or a French classical play, in which the audience sees none of the action
whatever, there is nothing but dialogue. Even in a
play as full of physical action and movement as *Antony and
Cleopatra*, *Dr. Faustus*, *The White Devil*, *The Revenger's
Tragedy* or *You Never Can Tell*, the dialogue still takes nearly
all the playing time. Thus a play can survive almost everything else—a clumsy and improbable plot, as in *The Duchess
of Malfi* or *All's Well That Ends Well*; a painful and disturbing theme[1] as in Ibsen's *Ghosts*, Strindberg's *The Father*, or
Bourdet's *The Prisoner*; types rather than characters, as in
Jonson's *The Alchemist*, Shaw's *The Apple Cart* and Vanbrugh's *The Provok'd Wife*; historical inaccuracies, as in
every historical play Shakespeare wrote and many other historical plays; overstatement of one side of a case, as in nearly
all plays with a political or religious theme; but a play with
many other merits cannot survive if the dialogue is hopelessly
non-speakable. Dr. Johnson, a most able man, well-read, a
great writer, perhaps a genius, tried his hand at a play,

[1] I do not mean that no plays with disturbing themes should be
written. Far from it. One of the functions of art is to shake compla-
cency; but such a play meets opposition.

97

Conventions

Irene, which, carefully written, dignified and bearing many evidences of a noble and thoughtful mind, is dead theatrically because the dialogue is over-formal, although in 1749 it was produced by Garrick and is said to have earned Dr. Johnson nearly £300. Chapman, whose translation of Homer thrilled Keats, wrote thirteen plays; his tragedies especially contain some magnificent language, but again they are somehow not actable. T. S. Eliot writes poetry that is very allusive, indirect and complex and requires careful and persistent study to yield up its full riches; but in his five plays, all successful in the theatre, he has wisely written dialogue that can immediately be taken in, at least on its upper level of meaning, and that can be spoken tolerably well even without long meditation; he has realized the difference between things to be read and things to be acted and has thus been successful in both art forms.

Here is an example of stilted and unreal dialogue:

Juba: Oh, Marcia, let me hope thy kind concern
And gentle wishes follow me to battle!
The thought will give new vigour to my arm,
And strength and weight to my descending sword,
And drive it in a tempest on the foe.

Marcia: My pray'rs and wishes always shall attend
The friends of Rome, the glorious cause of virtue,
And men approv'd of by the gods and Cato.

Juba: That Juba may deserve thy pious cares,
I'll gaze for ever on thy godlike father,
Transplanting one by one, into my life,
His bright perfections, 'till I shine like him.

Marcia: My father never, at a time like this,
Would lay out his great soul in words, and waste
Such precious moments.

Juba: Thy reproofs are just,
Thou virtuous maid; I'll hasten to my troops,
And fire their languid souls with Cato's virtue.
If e'er I lead them to the field, when all

98

The war shall stand rang'd in its just array,
And dreadful pomp; then will I think on thee.
Oh, lovely maid! then will I think on thee;
And in the shock of charging hosts, remember
What glorious deed should grace the man who hopes
For Marcia's love. (*Exit Juba*)

Lucia: Marcia, you're too severe;
How could you chide the young good-natur'd prince
And drive him from you with so stern an air,
A prince that loves and doats on you to death?

Marcia: 'Tis therefore, Lucia, that I chid him from me.
His air, his voice, his looks and honest soul,
Speak all so movingly in his behalf,
I dare not trust myself to hear him talk.

ADDISON: *Cato*

All very noble, no doubt; but neither human nor dramatic. It could be argued that this is blank verse, and that it is any-way unnatural to speak in blank verse, but we accept it in Shakespeare and several of his contemporaries, in T. S. Eliot or in Christopher Fry. Their verse dialogue is, however, more speakable and graceful; it is an intensification of human language, not a distortion; it may be more essentially realistic, though within an accepted artificial convention, than a piece of bad prose dialogue such as this:

Barnwell: Her disorder is so great, she don't perceive she has laid her hand on mine. Heav'ns! how she trembles!—What can this mean? (*Aside*)

Millwood: The interest I have in all that relates to you, (the reason of which you shall know hereafter) excites my curiosity; and were I sure you would pardon my presumption, I should desire to know your real sentiments on a very particular subject.

Barnwell: Madam, you may command my poor thoughts on any subject, I have none that I would conceal.

Conventions

Millwood: You'll think me bold.

Barnwell: No, indeed.

Millwood: What then are your thoughts of love?

Barnwell: If you mean the love of women, I have not thought of it at all. My youth and circumstances make such thoughts improper in me yet. But if you mean the general love we owe to mankind, I think no one has more of it in his temper than myself. I don't know that person in the world, whose happiness I don't wish, and would not promote, were it in my power. In an especial I love my uncle, and my master; but above all, my friend.

Millwood: You have a friend, then, whom you love?

Barnwell: As he does me, sincerely.

Millwood: He is, no doubt, often blessed with your company and conversation?

Barnwell: We live in one house, and both serve the same worthy merchant.

GEORGE LILLO: *George Barnwell*

For a long time this play was much esteemed for its moral value; but the conversation is so unlike that of normal human beings and so inartistic that even the moral hardly comes through.

The dialogue of a play must be such that the normally competent actor can speak his lines without stumbling, stopping for breath in the wrong place or speaking with so little animation or such a false intonation that it is obvious he does not understand what he is saying; it must also be such that the audience for whom the play is written can take in most of what is being said in the time available. These are essentials as much of the most trivial farce as of *King Lear*. Gracefulness of cadence is a merit; abundance of wit in comedy, glory of diction in tragedy, lucidity and speed of argument in the drama of ideas, human probability and individual idiom in the speech given to different characters, originality of phrase and vocabulary, vividness of description—these are all splendid things; but they are not essential to make a play a good practicable acting play, though some of them in some measure are to be found in every play that is worth studying.

One of the chief differences between a play and a novel is that every single fact or idea in a play has to be conveyed to the audience by someone *saying* it. The dramatist cannot, like Fielding or Jane Austen, step in with a word of explanation or an illuminating comment. He cannot usually find a letter or document more than once in the play without the risk of titters from an unsympathetic audience. He cannot let us know what is happening in the minds of characters by telling us in the third person, showing us the images that pass through their minds in sleep or reveries, making them keep a journal or any other of the other devices acceptable in the novel; and what can be told by direct, visible action is, as already stated, much limited by the size and shape of a stage and the physical capabilities of the actors, as well as by considerations of seemliness. For the most part we have to learn what is happening by listening to conversation.

This has several interesting results. One is that nearly all the characters in a play are amazingly talkative. They are for ever explaining things, justifying themselves, saying what they have just done or what they intend to do. They are often both more communicative and more articulate than most of us can or dare be. The soliloquy has already been mentioned. The communicativeness of theatrical characters may at times have an almost comic effect, though we should not let it have except for purposes of close analytical criticism. (There is something almost repellent as well as childish in the member of an audience who is looking for something ludicrous in a tragic play, who enjoys an actor's mishap—it is the vulgar mind that laughs *too* easily.) For example, when Richard III wants a murderer he merely calls a Page to his side and says in a sociable manner:

Conventions

Know'st thou not any whom corrupting gold
Would tempt unto a close exploit of death?
Richard III, Act IV, Sc. 2

I have never, so far, wished to engage the services of a murderer, but if I ever do I hope I shall have more sense than to proclaim my intentions to an immature, untried and probably irresponsible youngster.

We might compare this near-fatuity with the subtlety of Iago's use of Roderigo, to whom he tells plausible lies and at whose mercy he puts his own reputation. Again, in plays people in love are often given speeches of marvellous lyrical beauty; in real life people are often more inarticulate, perhaps from embarrassment, perhaps from humility, in declaring their love than at any other time in their lives. One of the pathetic things in life is the difficulty most of us have in expressing our tenderest feelings of love and friendship and even compassion, and the need others have to hear such expressions. People do sometimes come out with a few pretty expressions, but hardly with the passionate spate of a Portia, a Romeo or even Alizon and Richard in Christopher Fry's *The Lady's Not For Burning*. Even Henry V, who is conscious of being an uncourtly lover and says to Princess Katherine of France, 'I have no cunning in protestation', pours out long paragraphs of lively talk, wit and pleasant apology for his supposed inarticulateness, so that Katherine is justified in saying, 'Your majestee 'ave *fausse* French enough to deceive de most sage *demoiselle* dat is *en France*.' However, on the stage we might miss the significant raising of a would-be murderer's eyebrow, the sulky monosyllable of anger, the flush of modesty, the mutual glances of people in love; and the appeal of a scene of lyrical love on the stage is perhaps partly because the lovers say things we feel and would like to be able to say, but can ourselves usually express only in grunts and murmured endearments that, on the public stage, would be funny or embarrassing.

Part of this supernormal articulateness of persons in a

102

drama is also found in the speed with which things are explained. In two hours there is no time for the abundance of
irrelevant detail which most of us use when explaining something, or, except for special dramatic effect, for those tactful
hesitations, reticencies and circumlocutions we use when
playing a part in normal life. The pompous Dogberry, an
ignorant man fond of the sound of his own voice, is one of
the few characters in Shakespeare who does not say what he
wishes to say, because he cannot control language. This
makes him a delightful comic character; but if in real life
inability to say what one meant were comic most of us who
deal with other human beings would be in fits of laughter
many times a day. The clear, concise, unambiguous expression of what we want to say is an art that most of us have to
learn. Listen, in contrast, to Cressida, far from being one of
the greatest Shakespearian heroines:

> Hard to seem won: but I was won, my lord,
> With the first glance that ever—pardon me—
> If I confess much, you will play the tyrant.
> I love you now; but not, till now, so much
> But I might master it:—in faith, I lie;
> My thoughts were like unbridled children, grown
> Too headstrong for their mother:—see, we fools!
> Why have I blabb'd? Who shall be true to us
> When we are so unsecret to ourselves?—
> But, though I lov'd you well, I woo'd you not;
> And yet, good faith, I wisht myself a man,
> Or that we women had men's privilege
> Of speaking first. Sweet, bid me hold my tongue;
> For, in this rapture, I shall surely speak
> The thing I shall repent.
>
> *Troilus and Cressida*, Act III, Sc. 2

Millions of women must have felt something like this, but
few can express it as clearly and prettily. Again, there are
times when we would like to tell someone what we think of
them in a well-chosen and copious stream of invective. In

fact we generally have to stop after the first few bad names,
not from a return of amiability but from shortage of vocabulary. How satisfying it would sometimes be if we could talk
like this!

'Why doest thou converse with that trunk of humours,
that bolting-hutch of beastliness, that swoll'n parcel of
dropsies, that huge bombard of sack, that stuft cloakbag of
guts, that roasted Manningtree ox with the pudding in his
belly, that reverend vice, that gray iniquity, that father
ruffian, that vanity in years?'

Henry IV, Part I, Act II, Sc. 4

On the other hand, persons in a play are often more concise than in real life, because the dramatist has no time for
irrelevancies. A good example of this is to be found in the
stichomythia common in Greek drama, in which a passage of
argument or of question and answer, often on a very important subject, takes place with each person speaking alter-
nating single lines. When at the beginning of *Henry V* we are
treated to an excessively long and tedious account of the
operation of the Salic Law, an account which really does resemble a real political speech, we rightly resent it as bad
craftsmanship and in the film it was found necessary to cover
up the dullness of the speech with buffoonery. The following
brief explanation is much more artistic, though in fact it is
hardly likely that someone as sensible as Portia would cram
so much information into one short speech made to a
number of bewildered people:

> You are all amaz'd:
> Here is a letter, read it at your leisure;
> It comes from Padua, from Bellario:
> There shall you find that Portia was the doctor;
> Nerissa there her clerk: Lorenzo here
> Shall witness that I set forth soon as you,
> And even but now return'd; I have not yet
> Entered my house. Antonio, you are welcome;
> And I have better news in store for you

104

Than you expect: unseal this letter soon;
There you shall find three of your argosies
Are richly come to harbour suddenly:
You shall not know by what strange accident
I chanced upon this letter.

The Merchant of Venice, Act V, Sc. 1

As realism this leaves something to be desired; Portia explains a complicated intrigue in a very few words and then gives Antonio a piece of important news without telling him —indeed, refusing to tell him—probably because Shakespeare was in haste to finish his play and did not want to think of a good reason, what she is doing with a letter that belongs to him, and, really much more puzzling, how she knows what is in it when it is still sealed. Yet on the stage we notice nothing odd here. The facts that are dismissed quickly are those we already know; the barest acknowledgement is all that is now required. The news of Antonio's ships is told at rather more length, being fresh to us; but when listening to the play we receive this cheerful news gladly and do not trouble ourselves as to how Portia knows it.

Confidences and secrets are extracted quickly on the stage, simply because there is no time on the stage for the long persuasions usually needed in the home:

Penthea: Who is the saint you serve?[1]
Ithocles: Friendship, or nearness
Of birth to any but my sister, durst not
Have moved that question; 'tis a secret, sister,
I dare not murmur to myself.
Penthea: Let me,
By your new protestations I conjure you,
Partake her name.
Ithocles: Her name?—'tis—'tis I dare not.
Penthea: All your respects are forged.
Ithocles: They are not—Peace!

[1] That is, 'the lady you love'.

Conventions

Calantha is—the princess—the king's daughter—
Sole heir of Sparta.
JOHN FORD: *The Broken Heart*, Act III, Sc. 2

It would be sensible, in a discussion of character, to say that
Ithocles shows how much he loves and trusts his sister when
he tells her this dangerous secret. It would be unsound to say
that he shows a frivolous recklessness because he tells his
sister with so little persuasion; this is part of the practical
necessity of the drama. There is a similar very rapid confidence between two sisters in Wynyard Browne's *The Holly
and the Ivy*. People often talk very much more about their
past lives than we do in real life, because a confession is
often necessary to the understanding of a character. In early
plays this is often done with rather inadequate psychological
motives; in a modern play such a personal confession or
apologia is seldom made without some strong emotional
stimulus to provoke it. A fine example from a modern play
is the first of two moving personal statements made by the
schoolmaster Andrew Crocker-Harris to a young teacher in
Terence Rattigan's *The Browning Version*. Andrew makes
this confession, very unlike his normal habit of reticence,
when he is ill, tired, harassed and newly informed that he is
known as 'The Himmler of the Lower Fifth', a phrase which
comes as a shock to him:

Gilbert: I want to learn.
Andrew: I can only teach you from my own experience.
For two or three years I tried very hard to communicate to the boys some of my own joy in the
great literature of the past. Of course I failed, as
you will fail, nine hundred and ninety-nine times
out of a thousand. But a single success can atone,
and more than atone, for all the failures in the
world. And sometimes—very rarely, it is true—
but sometimes I had that success. That was in
the early years.

106

The Technique of Dialogue—Individuals

Gilbert: (*eagerly listening*) Please go on, sir.

Andrew: In early years, too, I discovered an easy substitute for popularity. (*He picks up his speech.*) I had of course acquired—we all do—many little mannerisms and tricks of speech, and I found that the boys were beginning to laugh at me. I was very happy at that, and encouraged the boys' laughter by playing up to it. It made our relationship so very much easier. They didn't like me as a man, but they found me funny as a character, and you can teach more things by laughter than by earnestness—for I never did have much sense of humour. So, for a time, you see, I was quite a success as a schoolmaster. . . . (*He stops.*) I fear this is all very personal and embarrassing to you. Forgive me. You need have no fears about the lower fifth. (*He puts the speech into his pocket and turns to the window.*)

(*Gilbert rises and moves above the desk.*)

Gilbert: (*after a pause*) I'm afraid I said something that hurt you very much. It's myself you must forgive, sir. Believe me, I'm desperately sorry.

Andrew: (*turning down stage and leaning slightly on the back of the swivel chair*) There's no need. You were merely telling me what I should have known for myself. Perhaps I did in my heart and hadn't the courage to acknowledge it. I knew, of course, that I was not only not liked, but positively disliked. I had realized too that the boys for many long years now—had ceased to laugh at me. I don't know why they no longer found me a joke. Perhaps it was my illness. No, I don't think it was that. Something deeper than that. Not sickness of the body, but a sickness of the soul. At all events it didn't take much discernment on my part to realize I had become an utter failure as a schoolmaster. Still, stupidly enough, I hadn't realized

107

Conventions

that I was also feared. 'The Himmler of the Lower Fifth.' I suppose that will become my epitaph.

Andrew makes an even more intimate personal statement to another young schoolmaster near the end of the play; the final confession more or less explains Andrew's pathetic and unlovable present character; but it is not a confession a man of his temperament would easily make; it is made to seem natural by the fact that he has previously been shaken by this conversation with Gilbert, by an unexpected kindness from a pupil and by a particularly cruel and senseless piece of disloyalty from his wife. We have already seen him give way under the strain and weep.

An important aspect of dialogue is the differentiation of the speech of individuals. Every speech, at least ideally, is characteristic of the speaker. Completely realistic representation of personal idioms would be dull. Many people do not talk in sentences. People who are shy, uneducated or unintelligent do not often talk in sentences; and many of the human race come into one of these three categories. No one talks in sentences all the time: animal grunts, one-word answers to questions, unfinished sentences, slovenly grammar, ellipses, vulgarisms, vague remarks, polite formula, are all found in abundance even in the normal conversation of cultured people. Wit is rare even in people blessed with a sense of humour. A play, then, in which everyone spoke the exact language of contemporary ordinary speech would drag, irritate and be unbearably dull. The plays of Shakespeare and his contemporaries, or of Christopher Fry, make no attempt at such sterile realism but show enjoyment of splendid diction. But it is equally true that in plays coming nearer to the naturalistic, such as those of James Bridie, J. M. Barrie, John Galsworthy, Noel Coward, J. B. Priestley or Somerset Maugham, the speech is still much terser, more vivid, more epigrammatic and more eloquent than that of real people.

In drama speech must, we see, be more attractive and economical than it is in real life; this is, fortunately, made to seem more natural by the fact that drama, whether tragedy or comedy, usually has as its subject a portion of life in which critical events are happening and the emotions involved are indeed somewhat stronger than those felt when making toast or catching the 8.15. In fact important events and violent emotions often render even articulate persons quite incapable of expression, or inadequate at least; but they do also sometimes stimulate and enliven speech, and we are prepared to accept the latter as the likelier probability in a play. Much of the finest drama is poetic, of course, and we do not usually speak poetry at all. This problem will be discussed later in a chapter to itself; but for the moment let me say only that for ordinary people to speak poetry in a play is no more unnatural than for them all to speak much more clearly, fluently and gracefully than is likely in real life; drama is, as it is one of the purposes of this book to stress, a mass of accepted conventions; and drama as we know it would be impossible if actors on the stage spoke as badly, even in the physical sense, as the average person does in the home.

However, even when we realize that for the purposes of drama the standard of everyone's speech has to be raised, we feel that there should be some differentiation, and this giving of individual speech characteristics to at least the important individuals in a play is one of the arts that distinguishes a good dramatist from a mediocre one. Speech is, in real life, a considerable clue to social positions, standards of education, character and habits; if the snob value that has attached itself to some of the most pleasing English is to be deplored, it cannot be denied, and the best democratization of language would be for all to learn to speak standard English. These distinctions remain in the drama, though usually either sharpened or blunted according to the necessities of the play. Shaw's *Pygmalion* is a play in which this social significance of speech is the central theme, and speech is therefore very much differentiated. There is a great deal of difference, indicative of educational standing and social

Conventions

rank, in the speech of Dogberry and Leonato (*Much Ado About Nothing*), Juliet and her Nurse (*Romeo and Juliet*) or Ernest and Mrs. Conway (J. B. Priestley's *Time and the Conways*). These differences are a matter not only of pronunciation, but of the choice of words, sentence-structure, tact or the lack of it, explicitness, delicacy of language or otherwise and all the other qualities that go to make up a person's speech habits. Yet, whereas in almost everything else drama heightens the qualities and individualities found in real life, in the matter of speech habits of this kind it may have to reduce the distinction somewhat; there is not much scope in drama for the very inarticulate, people with speech impediments (the occasional ridicule of stammerers on the stage is little short of wicked!) or even very reserved and laconic people; the extremes of dialect and of professional jargon are understood by a few only; those too numerous people who speak mostly in clichés and catch-phrases can be treated only as comic figures, though such people are not exempt in real life from tragic or profound experience; and those often harmless and amiable enough people whose language is very coarse cannot be accurately represented on the stage.

Various kinds of individuality can be given to speech. There is the magnificent imagery of Othello, who is perhaps meant to show some of the gorgeousness of an Oriental imagination. There is the bluff worldly style of Iago, resembling in some ways that of Edmund in *King Lear*. There is Richard the Second's habitual and apparently conscious cultivation of beautiful and figurative speech, carried so far as to become a defect of character; he is a tragic sentimentalist, playing with words when he should be acting and reasoning, whereas the Duke Orsino in *Twelfth Night* is a prettily comic one. In tragedy and historical drama we may notice the ineffectual sententiousness and circumlocution of Polonius and the slow repetitive manner of the Grave-digger in *Hamlet*: the flowery liveliness and inventiveness of Mercutio with his fancy, contrasted with the deeper lyricism of

110

Romeo, with his brooding imagination, in *Romeo and Juliet*;
the manly vigour and deliberate tactlessness of Philip Faul-
conbridge in *King John*; Hotspur's impulsiveness in speech
as in action in *Henry IV*, Part I;[1] Casca's habit of sarcasm
and irony and Mark Antony's organized rhetoric in *Julius
Caesar*; the nasty images of Thersites in *Timon of Athens*;
Isabella's fastidiousness in speech and dislike of eloquence
in *Measure for Measure*—a play which has certainly a con-
ventionally happy ending, but cannot be reckoned a comedy
in the real sense—and so on.

The tragic or serious treatment of individual speech will
be concerned mostly with imagery and the quality of imagination, those aspects of speech that really show something
of the inner personality; in comedy the differences of speech
are often more the superficial distinctions of mannerisms.
The peculiarities of Mrs. Malaprop come to mind:

'Oh! it gives me the hydrostatics to such a degree.—I
thought she had persisted from corresponding with him; but
behold, this very day, I have interceded another letter from
the fellow.'

SHERIDAN: *The Rivals*, Act III, Sc. 3

Shakespeare seems to have been as much conscious of the
comic possibilities of speech mannerisms as he was of the
deeper significance of images: we have the pedantry of
Holofernes:

'You find not the apostrophes, and so miss the accent; let
me supervise the canzonet. Here are only numbers ratified;
but, for the elegancy, facility and golden cadence of poetry,
caret. Ovidius Naso was the man: and why, indeed, Naso,
but for smelling out the odoriferous flowers of fancy, the
jerks of invention? Imitari is nothing: so doth the hound his
master, the ape his keeper, the tired horse his rider.'

Love's Labour's Lost, Act IV, Sc. 2

[1] Sir Laurence Olivier played this part with a stammer on 'w' which
seemed very appropriate to the character.

Conventions

the pseudo-elegancies of Osric:

'Sir, here is newly come to court Laertes; believe me, an absolute gentleman, full of most excellent differences, of very soft society and great showing: indeed, to speak feelingly of him, he is in the card or calendar of gentry, for you shall find in him the continent of what a gentleman should be.

Hamlet, Act V, Sc. 2

Welsh cadences:

'There is occasions and causes why and wherefore in all things; I will tell you, asse my friend, Captain Gower:—the rascally, scald, peggarly, lousy, pragging knave, Pistol— which you and yourself, and all the 'orld, know to be no petter than a fellow, look you now, of no merits,—he is come to me, and prings me pread and salt yesterday, look you, and pid me eat my leek: it was in a place where I could preed no contentions with him; but I will be so pold as to wear it in my cap till I see him once again, and then I will tell him a little piece of my desires.'

FLUELLEN, in *Henry V*, Act V, Sc. 1

French accents, Scots accents, blustering mannerisms borrowed from earlier plays, fashionable slang and mannerisms, Euphuism—a fashionable prose style of the day,—childish prattle, the ravings of lunacy. Falstaff has a very characteristic mode of speech:

'Bardolph, am I not fallen away vilely since this last action? do I not bate? do I not dwindle? Why, my skin hangs about me like an old lady's loose gown; I am withered like an old apple-john. Well, I'll repent, and that suddenly, while I am in some liking; I shall be out of heart shortly, and then I shall have no strength to repent. An I have not forgotten what the inside of a church is made of, I am a peppercorn, a brewer's horse! the inside of a church! Company, villainous company, hath been the spoil of me.'

Henry IV, Part I, Act III, Sc. 3

The Technique of Dialogue—Individuals

This is imitated quite cleverly in W. Kenrich's readable comedy *Falstaff's Wedding*, into which he brings most of the comic characters to be found with Falstaff in Shakespeare's plays:

Falstaff: I would I were in East-cheap. Mine hostess hath a most excellent cordial; and I never stood in more need of it than now. The gross indignity Hal hath put on me, sticks in my throat, and in the end, may go near to choak me. I shall never gulp it down: that's flat; unless, indeed, a full cup of sherris help to clear the way. And then, how I shall stomach it; how I shall digest it, Heaven knows! At present both my person and my knighthood are in jeopardy; my lord chief justice, to whose care I am commended, holding me not altogether in good liking. But no matter if I am to be provided for, what avails it who is my caterer? I could wish, nevertheless, old white wine stood higher in his lordship's favour, that I may not be stinted at table, or in my by-drinkings. I like not such splenetic temperaments; such phlegmatic constitutions; grey-beards, that never make allowances for the continual waste of radical moisture.—'Sblood, I am as foundered and as sore as a blind horse in a mill. Bardolph! where a plague art thou gotten to, caterwauling!

Other dramatists have made use of national speech mannerisms; the refugee with a foreign accent of some kind is quite a common figure in contemporary drama. Here is a stage Irishman from an eighteenth-century play:

Careless: Have you paid the money I sent you with?
Teague: Yes, but I will carry no more, look you there, now.
Careless: Why, Teague?
Teague: God sa' my shoul now, I shall run away with it.
Careless: Pish, thou art too honest.

Conventions

Teague: That I am too upon my shoul now; but the devil
is not honest, that he is not; he would not let me
alone when I was going; but he made me go to
this little long place, and t'other little long place;
and upon my shoul was carrying me to Ireland,
for he made me go by a dirty place like a lough
now; and therefore I know now it was the way to
Ireland. Then I would stand still, and then he
would make me go on; and then I would go to
one side, and he would make me go to t'other
side; and then I got a little farther, and did run
then; and upon my shoul the devil could not
catch me; and then I did pay the money: but I
will carry no money, that I will not.

Careless: But thou sha't, Teague, when I have more to
send; thou art proof now against temptation.

Teague: Well then, if you send me with the money again,
and I do not come to thee upon the time, the devil
will make me begone then with the money.

SIR R. HOWARD: *The Committee*

A better-known stage Irishman is Foigard in Farquhar's
The Beaux' Stratagem.

What might be called professional idiom is also useful,
generally for comic effect; there are many stage doctors,
some suave and sinister, some gentle and soothing, some
eccentric. Barré Lyndon's *The Amazing Dr. Clitterhouse*, in
which the hero is a doctor who plunges into crime out of
scientific curiosity about the reactions of criminals, achieves
a number of startling or comic effects by the sudden use of
dignified professional medical terms about such things as
blood-pressure or laryngeal spasms in the midst of episodes
of crime and violence. Dr. Knox of James Bridie's *The Anatomist* uses some medical jargon, though his idiom is more
personal than professional. The language of the school staff-
room is found in several modern plays. Here is a sailor from
an eighteenth-century play:

The Technique of Dialogue—Individuals

Colonel Evans: My father in London! you surprise me, captain—What can have brought him here?

Captain: Nay, as to the matter of surprise, my young hero, your father was quite as much astonished at hearing of your being in the same port, as you can be; and as to your aunt Winifred, she stared with as much amazement, as the sailors that spied the first Patagonian. Your sister, indeed, seemed more pleased than any of them, at the news, and inquired whether I had met you in healthy condition, and if I knew your moorings.

Colonel: My gentle Harriot!—I am impatient to see her.

Captain: Hoist sail, and away, then; I'll be your convoy, though I should like better to drop anchor, and take in refreshment for an hour or so, at the Admiralty Coffee-House, where I have appointed Captain Blast of the Boreas, and some other jolly lads to meet me.

MRS. ELIZABETH GRIFFITHS: *The School for Rakes*

Zeal-of-the-Land Busy, a Puritan, in Jonson's *Bartholomew Fair*, uses the canting language of the extreme Puritans; and Kastril, the Angry Boy of his *The Alchemist*, the fashionable language of a wild young man prone to duels and quarrels. Fashionable speech mannerisms are often mocked in modern plays; unfortunately this form of satire tends to date quickly. Here is an incurable gossip from the same set of characters as Teague:

Mrs. Day: And now you talk of this same Abel, I tell you but one thing:—I wonder that neither he nor my husband's honour's chief clerk, Obadiah, is not here ready to attend me. I dare warrant my son Abel has been here two hours before us: 'Tis the veriest Princox; he will ever be gallopping, and

Conventions

yet he is not full one and twenty, for all his ap-
pearances. He never stole this trick of gallopping; his father was just such another before
him, and would gallop with the best of 'em: he,
and Mrs. Busie's husband, were counted the best
horsemen in Reading—ay, and Berkshire to
boot. I have rode formerly behind Mr. Busie, but
in truth I cannot now endure to travel but in a
coach; my own is, at present, in disorder, and
so I was fain to shift in this:—but I warrant you,
if his honour, Mr. Day, chairman of the honourable committee of sequestration, should know
that his wife rode in a stage-coach, he would
make the house too hot for some.—Why, how
is't with you, sir? What, weary of your journey?
(*To the Colonel*)

Blunt: Her tongue will never tire. (*Aside*) —So many,
mistress, riding in the coach, has a little distem-
per'd me with heat.

Mrs. Day: So many, sir! why there were but six—What
would you say if I should tell you that I was one
of the eleven that travell'd at one time in one
coach?

Blunt: Oh, the devil, I have given her a new theme.
(*Aside*)

SIR R. HOWARD: *The Committee*

Perhaps, lest the reader should be tempted to make the
same comment as Blunt, it may be as well to postpone the
discussion of the use of poetry and prose for different characters, in the Shakespearian period and occasionally later, until
the general functions of poetry and prose in drama are discussed; and we will turn from the speeches that make up
dialogue to the pattern of dialogue.

VIII. THE TECHNIQUE OF DIALOGUE—CONVERSATION

One dissertates, he is candid;
Two must discept—has distinguished;
Three helps the couple, if ever yet man did;
Four protests; Five makes a dart at the thing wished:
Back to One, goes the case bandied.

ROBERT BROWNING: *Master Hugues of Saxe-Gotha*

IT would theoretically be possible—I do not know if it has ever happened—for a play to be written in which every speech was suited with wondrous subtlety to an individual, imagined character, and every speech was, in itself, speakable and agreeable to hear, but the play could not be produced because the dialogue as strung together bore no resemblance to real conversation. Perhaps in a sense Shelley's *Prometheus Unbound* is an example of this.

Certainly conversations in a play have marked differences from conversations in real life. The differences in single speeches have been mentioned above. In dialogue there are fewer interruptions; people do not, except for special comic effect, bore other people; almost everyone is a more attentive and courteous listener than in real life, though, of course, the quality of the talk makes boredom less likely. Unless for some special comic or pathetic effect, people are much less concerned with such practical, immediate necessities as going out to work, cleaning boots, bathing the baby and catching the post; and no dazzling conversation or intimate confidence is ever interrupted, as so often happens in real life, by someone's needing urgently to attend to a natural necessity! The conversation is generally more fairly shared than among live persons in a room in real life. There may

117

be a scene in a play in which a large number of people all sit in a group informally discussing a subject, as in Bernard Shaw's *Getting Married*, when in real life they would probably have split up into smaller groups, all talking on topics of urgent interest to them. Producers of the plays of Shakespeare and his contemporaries and of other plays in which a large number of characters is present on the stage simultaneously, often find that during a longish conversation between two members of the group it is best to let the other persons fall into groups apart and pretend to be engaged in conversations of their own in the background.

Another convention of stage dialogue is the 'aside', a way of showing inner thoughts as opposed to outward expression:

Julius Caesar: Bid them prepare within:—
I am to blame to be thus waited for.—
Now, Cinna:—now, Metellus:—what, Trebonius!
I have an hour's talk in store for you:
Remember that you call on me today:
Be near me, that I may remember you.

Trebonius: Caesar, I will:—(*aside*) and so near will I be,
That your best friends will wish I had been further.

Julius Caesar, Act II, Sc. 2

Standard: I once, madam, hoped the honour of defending you from all injuries, through a title to your lovely person, but now my love must attend my fortune. My commission, madam, was my passport to the fair; adding a nobleness to my passion, it stampt a value on my love; 'twas once the life of honour, but now its winding sheet, and with it must my love be buried.

Parly: What, disbanded, colonel?
Faugh, the nauseous fellow! he stinks of poverty already. (*Aside*)

The Technique of Dialogue—Conversation

Lurewell: His misfortune troubles me, because it may prevent my designs. (*Aside*)

GEORGE FARQUHAR: *The Constant Couple*

By the standards of absolute realism—impossible in any art —this is idiotic. Caesar is in the frame of mind to be on the watch for anything suspicious. His wife has had an alarming dream which, together with a storm, has kept him awake; he has been persuaded not to go to the Capitol and now Decius Brutus has persuaded him to change his mind. Though a brave and dignified man, he is apt to be superstitious and he is very nervous at present (he is an epileptic); it might be expected that he would notice Trebonius muttering to himself in a sinister fashion. Yet he goes on talking sociably without any awkward questions. Similarly, a sudden descent into poverty usually makes a man very sensitive to evidence of the constancy or otherwise of his former friends, and it is unlikely that Colonel Standard would fail to hear comments calculated to arouse his suspicions. In real life most of us are not so fortunate as to be able to relieve our feelings by muttering to ourselves in the presence of the people we object to; if we try to, the enemy is sure to say, 'And what is that you are saying?' Even deaf people have an uncanny gift for noticing something we say when we would rather they did not. But the 'aside' is accepted on the stage as a means of showing that what one character says to another is insincere or has a double meaning. It is used very little in the more naturalistic twentieth-century drama.

However, though drama is a heightened, not a photographic, representation of life—a purely realistic portrayal would give no pleasure—it must give the *illusion* of reality when we are watching it, unless it is frank fantasy or sensationalism.

The extreme concentration of drama makes this packing of much information into a few lines of dialogue frequently needful. The reader can easily find several hundred examples. However, dramatic dialogue may also be less con-

119

Conventions

centrated than normal speech, in the sense that it is more rhetorical[1] and embroiders upon its theme. The best living example of this is Christopher Fry, with his wonderful richness and originality of language. It is delightful to hear people talking like this, though we do not do it ourselves in the home:

Tyson:	All right, yes, all right, all right. Now why Can't people mind their own business? This shooting star Has got nothing to do with us, I am quite happy In my mind about that. It probably went past Perfectly preoccupied with some astral anxiety or other Without giving us a second thought. Eh, Tappercoom? One of those quaint astrological holus-boluses, Quite all right.
Tappercoom:	Quite. An excess of phlegm. In the solar system. It was on its way To a heavenly spittoon. How is that, How is that? On its way—
Tyson:	I consider it unwise To tempt Providence with humour, Tappercoom.
Margaret:	And on the one evening when we expect company! What company is going to venture to get here Through all that heathen hullabaloo in the road? Except the glorious company of the Apostles, And we haven't enough glasses for all that number.

The Lady's Not for Burning, Act II

A play often contains a number of great set speeches in

[1] Not in the current bad sense of the word.

120

The Technique of Dialogue—Conversation

prose or verse. These are dictated partly—in good drama—
by the passion and creative joy of the writer; but we should
not forget that they are also there to give the great actor
or actress an opportunity to show skill and fervour in the
handling of emotion. Such are the soliloquies of Hamlet and
Macbeth, the address to Helen and the great final speech of
Dr. Faustus, the comic soliloquies of Malvolio and Falstaff,
the great *tirades* of Racine, the speech beginning, 'Yes, they
told me you were fools'. In the last act of *Saint Joan*, the
Vicar's sermon in *The Dog Beneath the Skin* and Becket's
sermon in *Murder in the Cathedral*. Actors and actresses are
glad to have parts that give full scope to their virtuosity, and
dramatists generally seek to provide such opportunities;
Shakespeare and his contemporaries, and Shaw, are particularly generous in this.

The handling of dialogue modifies the speed of the drama.
In general, a scene with a few long speeches seems to move
in a slower and more stately manner than one in which the
speeches are short and come in quick succession. Here is a
fragment which begins with two long speeches to express the
languid, sentimental attachment of the King to his undesirable favourite and the favourite's sugary flattery, continues to sarcastic ceremony and gathers great speed with a
succession of one- or two-line speeches as the threat of
violence develops:

Edward: My Gaveston! welcome to Tynemouth! welcome
        to thy friend!
        Thy absence made me droop and pine away;
        For, as the lovers of fair Danae,
        When she was locked up in a brazen tower,
        Desired her more, and waxed outrageous,
        So did it fare with me: and now thy sight
        Is sweeter far than was thy parting hence
        Bitter and irksome to my sobbing heart.
Gaveston: Sweet lord and king, your speech preventeth
        mine,

121

Yet have I words left to express my joy:
The shepherd nipt with biting winter's rage
Frolics not more to see the painted spring
Than I do to behold your majesty.

Edward: Will none of you salute my Gaveston?

Lancaster: Salute him? yes; welcome, Lord Chamberlain!

Young Mortimer: Welcome is the good Earl of Cornwall!

Warwick: Welcome, Lord Governor of the Isle of Man!

Pembroke: Welcome Master Secretary!

Kent: Brother, do you hear them?

Edward: Still will these earls and barons use me thus.

Gaveston: My lord, I cannot brook these injuries.

Queen: (*aside*) Ah me, poor soul, when these begin to jar.

Edward: Return it to their throats, I'll be thy warrant.

Gaveston: Base, leaden earls, that glory in your birth,
Go sit at home and eat your tenants' beef;
And come not here to scoff at Gaveston,
Whose mounting thoughts did never creep so low
As to bestow a look on such as you.

Lancaster: Yet I disdain not to do this for you. (*Draws*)

Edward: Treason, treason! where's the traitor!

Pembroke: Here! here! king!
Convey hence Gaveston, they'll murder him.

Gaveston: The life of thee shall salve this foul disgrace.

Young Mortimer: Villain! thy life, unless I miss my aim.
(*Offers to stab him.*)

Queen: Ah, furious Mortimer, what hast thou done?

Young Mortimer: No more than I would answer, were he slain.

MARLOWE: *Edward II*, Act I, Sc. 2

We may contrast the longer and slower speeches of quiet discussion:

The Technique of Dialogue—Conversation

Young
Mortimer: Fair Isabel, now have we our desire,
           The proud corrupters of the light-brained King
           Have done their homage to the lofty gallows
           And he himself lies in captivity.
           Be ruled by me, and we will rule the realm,
           In any case take heed of childish fear,
           For now we hold an old wolf by the ears,
           That if he slip will seize upon us both,
           And gripe the sorer, being gript himself.
           Think therefore, madam, it imports us much
           To erect your son with all the speed we may,
           And that I be protector over him;
           For our behoof, 'twill bear the greater sway
           When as a king's name shall be underwrit.

Queen: Sweet Mortimer, the life of Isabel,
           Be thou persuaded that I love thee well,
           And therefore, so the prince my son be safe,
           Whom I esteem as dear as these mine eyes,
           Conclude against his father what thou wilt,
           And I myself will willingly subscribe.

Edward II, Act V, Sc. 2

The dignified slowness of the lyrical choruses in Greek drama and the speed of stichomythia may also be mentioned in this context. In general the dialogue of comedy moves more quickly than that of tragedy, though in comedy there is often less action or at least less momentous action.

In studying the craftsmanship of a given play we must notice the difference between dialogue whose first function is to convey information, to carry on the plot, and dialogue whose first function is to please by its beauty, wit, oddity or other intrinsic quality. A too thorough separation of these functions denotes bad dramatic craftsmanship, for much material is wasted in one sense or another and there is little room for waste in a two-hour play; but there is often some degree of division. Here, for instance, is an amusing passage

Conventions

of dialogue which also brings in some information vital to the development of the play:

Prince: I invented the small buffer-state of Neo-Slavonia. I invented all of it. Its name, its people, its customs, its orders and its literature. I then gave myself the title of Prince in that country. Who but I had the right to bestow that title? Whom more worthy of it than myself could I find?

Jennifer: (*nodding*) Prince Michael Robulski.

Prince: Robolski. In Neo-Slavonia the termination—ulski is now obsolete.

Jennifer: I must try to remember.

Prince: It's a jolly little country. You must let me show it to you one day.

Jennifer: Thank you. But would it be quite proper for us to go about together?

Prince: Proper?

Jennifer: The late General James Bulger,—C.B.—was very old-fashioned. I don't think he would like his widow—How do they regard these things in your country?

Prince: Ah, now tell me. I have been longing to ask you all the evening—only it sounded so absurd. Was there ever a General James Bulger—C.B.?

Jennifer: (*shocked*) Good heavens, no! You don't suggest that I'm a common bigamist, do you?

Prince: I wondered. Aren't you?

Jennifer: (*with dignity*) Certainly not.

Prince: I'm glad.

Jennifer: Besides, where would be the fun? I am an inventor.

Prince: I see.

Jennifer: I invented a big, red-faced soldier called Bulger. I invented all of him. I invented his rank, and his orders, and his medals. I then married him. Who but I had any right to consider myself as his wife?

A. A. MILNE: *To Have the Honour*, Act II

124

The Technique of Dialogue—Conversation

This is obviously indispensable to the whole plot of the play. Here, from the same play, is a piece of dialogue that, with the possible exception of Angela's line about the secretary, serves simply to amuse and delight by its humour, humanity and kindly repartee. It should be explained that Jennifer, a charming, lively lady, is 'so overflowing with vitality that some of it has got into her figure'.

Angela: It is ridiculous of you to pretend that you're fat. Why do you?

Jennifer: I don't. No woman pretends she's fat. But every woman over thirty is afraid. On her thirtieth birthday she starts looking at herself in the glass, and saying, 'Is it, or is it not?' And a morning comes when she says, 'I wonder.' I said it this morning. I say, where *is*—wherever it is?

Angela: Neo-Slavonia? I don't know. (*With a wave of her cigarette*) Down at the bottom on the right, I suppose. Somewhere.

Jennifer: They make geography so quickly nowadays that I can't keep up with it.

Angela: A sort of buffer-state. (*She gives Jennifer her earrings.*) There's a dear. I shall make a mess of my hair.

Jennifer: (*fixing them*) If one has never heard of a country one always calls it 'a sort of buffer-state'. 'Miss Angela Battersby was wearing the family drops.' It must be difficult to feel very patriotic about a country which is only used so as to prevent two other countries from getting at each other. . . . Other ear.

Angela: (*turning round*) It's never difficult to feel very patriotic.

Jennifer: True. At least, it's never difficult to feel how very unpatriotic other people are. . . . My buffer, 'tis of thee! . . . Is he very good-looking?

Angela: Not bad.

Conventions

Jennifer: And, to get down to my own class, what's the secretary like? . . . There!

Angela: (*looking at herself in the glass*) Thanks. . . . We haven't seen him. The Prince wrote to say that he was in London. Could he—and so on? I said, Delighted. Then he wrote that he and his secretary were at the Bull at Medenham. Could they—and so forth? I said, Of course. I suppose he's a sort of courier, equerry, orderly, or whatever you call it. I must go and finish myself. (*She goes.*)

Jennifer: Well, speaking as a widow with no desire to marry again, I wish you luck.

Angela: (*smiling mysteriously at her from half-way up the stairs*) Don't be vulgar, Jennifer.

Jennifer: I like being vulgar. It suits my shape. Anyhow, darling, promise that I shall be the first to hear.

Angela: You're sure to be, I should think. You're quite capable of hiding behind a tree, and listening. (*She goes into her room.*)

Jennifer: (*complacently*) I am. (*Surveying herself*) And thank you for 'tree', darling. I was afraid you were going to say 'bush' or 'clump'.

To Have the Honour, Act I

The only possible way to analyse a stage dialogue adequately is to act it, or, failing that, to read it aloud; if this is quite impossible one should at least read it aloud in imagination. There may be magnificent pieces of prose or poetry which are fine as compositions but quite impossible as dramatic speech, such as the plays of George Chapman; there may, on the other hand, be dramatic speeches of apparently poor literary quality which, when spoken aloud, show their merit for the practical purposes of the stage. Moreover, many broken speeches, hesitations, ambiguous expressions and animal noises take on an interesting significance on the stage. The person who wants to succeed in playreading should learn to laugh and cry on the stage at will, for one literal pronunciation of such conventional signs as 'Bohoo!' or 'Ha, ha!' can make a good dramatic dialogue sound wholly ridiculous and embarrassing.

Similarly we should not assume that a piece of dramatic dialogue is non-speakable simply because we cannot speak it well, if we are ourselves poor speakers in ordinary life. One of the very valuable results of education through drama is that it improves the standard of speech; people for very shame try to speak better and move with more dignity. There is no excuse for grossly bad speech nowadays, with many good books on speech training and plenty of competent teachers available; people who really do not value good speech and are incapable of learning to value it have no business to be studying plays, which are essentially organizations of aesthetically pleasing *talk*.

IX. VERSE AND PROSE IN DRAMA

> We wonder how the devil this difference grows
> Betwixt our fools in verse, and yours in prose.
> DRYDEN: Epilogue to *All for Love*

THERE are poetic dramas, such as T. S. Eliot's *The Family Reunion*, Christopher Fry's *Venus Observed* and *The Firstborn*, W. B. Yeats's *The Shadowy Waters*, the great Greek tragedies, the tragedies of Racine and Corneille, some of the plays of Victor Hugo, Goethe's *Faust*; there are tragedies written entirely in prose, such as Chekov's *Ivanov*, Gordon Daviot's *Richard of Bordeaux*, Somerset Maugham's *The Letter*, Shaw's *Saint Joan*; there are hundreds of comedies written in prose, such as Goldsmith's *She Stoops to Conquer*, Congreve's *The Way of the World*, J. B. Priestley's *Laburnum Grove*, Sheridan's *The Rivals*, Wilde's *The Importance of Being Earnest*, J. M. Barrie's *Dear Brutus*. There are a great many plays written partly in prose and partly in verse—we had better use the term *verse*, as even the finest dramatic poetry may include non-poetic lines that are merely metrical—these include all the plays of Shakespeare except *King John*, *Richard II* and the first and third parts of *Henry VI*, which are entirely in verse[1] and the classification includes hundreds of plays by contemporaries of Shakespeare; this mixture, though not nowadays common, is still not unheard of, being found in such worth-while plays as *Murder in the Cathedral* and Spender's *Trial of a Judge*. There are also plays in which the medium is a kind of highly stylized prose whose technique approaches poetry; examples of this are Oscar Wilde's

[1] The extent of Shakespeare's authorship in this trilogy is open to dispute.

Verse and Prose in Drama

Salome (originally written in French, and translated not by
Wilde but by Lord Alfred Douglas), J. M. Synge's *Deidre of
the Sorrows* and James Elroy Flecker's *Hassan*, which has
also verse interludes between scenes. A large book could
thus be written on the uses of prose and verse in the drama;
but the least experienced student can appreciate something
of the distinctions.

All drama is more dramatic than life, or is a selection of
the most dramatic portions of life; but poetry in drama implies that the play is removed one step further from literal
realism. It may not be as far from inner truthfulness as a
prose play; *Hamlet*, which is mostly in verse rising often
to great heights of dramatic poetry, is much nearer to the
truth about human minds than some commercial farce; but
the mode of speech does not imitate common speech so
closely. We might say, at the risk of seeming sentimental,
that in poetic drama souls are conversing, with an intimate
inner truth, and that in prose drama the normal outward
masks that most of us present to the world are conversing;
and, since we know only one person's inner life at all, our
own, and that not accurately, we can grasp a prose drama
more fully at a first hearing than *Lear* or *Othello*, *Medea* or
Antigone.

This is not true of all verse drama. For historical and
psychological reasons, the most primitive literature of a
culture generally seems to take the form of verse, and most
early British drama was written in some kind of verse, but
this seldom rose to the heights we know as poetry. The
Miracle Plays were mostly in simple verse which sometimes
touches a modern audience by its simplicity; an early farce
like *Gammer Gurton's Needle* (first printed 1575), is in verse,
but this, though vigorous and amusing, is not poetry:

Hodge: Daintrels diccon (gogs soule man) save this pece of
          dry horsbred,
          Cha byt no byt this lyue longe daie, no crome come
          in my hed

My gutts they yawle crawle and all my belly rum-
bleth
The puddynges can not lye still, ech one ouer other
tumbleth
By gogs harte cham so vexte, and in my belly pende
Chould one peece were at the spittlehouse another
at ye castels ende.

Modern pantomime also sometimes uses crude verse. To
claim such pieces as plays in which there is a profound insight into the human soul or a radiant heightening of human
experience would be ridiculous. An examination of *Titus
Andronicus* or of many plays by the lesser contemporaries of
Shakespeare soon demonstrates that it is just as possible to
have downright bad plays—plain bad, inarticulate, crude,
unreal, clumsy plays!—in pedestrian or disorganized blank
verse as in prose.

Even in the best plays of the Elizabethan period there are
passages of blank verse which might equally well, or perhaps
better, have been written in good prose:

Aegeon: My youngest boy, and yet my eldest care,
          At eighteen years became inquisitive
          After his brother; and importuned me
          That his attendant—so his case was like
          Reft of his brother, but retain'd his name—
          Might bear him company in the quest of him:
          Whom whilst I laboured of a love to see,
          I hazarded the loss of whom I loved.
          Five summers have I spent in furthest Greece,
          Roaming clean through the bounds of Asia,
          And, coasting homeward, came to Ephesus;
          Hopeless to find, yet loth to leave unsought
          Or that, or any place that harbours men.
          But here must end the story of my life;
          And happy were I in my timely death,
          Could all my travels warrant me they live.
                    The Comedy of Errors, Act I, Sc. 1

Verse and Prose in Drama

Though this is not one of Shakespeare's best plays, it is a good play of its period. The extract given above is a clear, sensible statement of something we need to know, but in no way is the matter beyond the capacities of prose. In the very next scene of this play we find a few lines of pathos that justify the use of verse with a real image, a truly creative moment:

Antipholus of Syracuse:

> He that commends me to mine own content
> Commends me to the thing I cannot get.
> I in the world am like a drop of water,
> That in the ocean seeks another drop;
> Who, failing there to find his fellow forth,
> Unseen, inquisitive, confounds himself;

and a few seconds later the heightening effect of verse is equally suitable for exuberant humour:

Dromio of Ephesus:

> Return'd so soon! rather approacht too late;
> The capon burns, the pig falls from the spit;
> The clock hath strucken twelve upon the bell,—
> My mistress made it one upon my cheek:
> She is so hot, because the meat is cold;
> The meat is cold, because you come not home;
> You come not home, because you have no stomach;
> You have no stomach, having broke your fast;
> But we, that know what 'tis to fast and pray
> Are penitent for your default today.

Neither of these is great poetry, but the passages serve to show that verse can do what prose cannot do.

The matter I hint at in the phrase 'inner truth' is more difficult to discuss. Perhaps in this function the use of true poetry in the drama can best be explained by a reference to the inadequacy of language. Few people have altogether escaped the experience of being in a situation in which the words they are able to produce seem hopelessly insufficient for the situation. Anyone who has had to write a letter of condolence to a bereaved intimate knows this feeling; we are also hampered by the insufficiency of our speech when confronted with great beauty, revolting ugliness, intense and visible suffering or an act of outstanding nobility or horrifying wickedness. Most of us have witnessed, if we have not felt, the choking inarticulateness of great anger or great grief; and joy can reach such extremes that we weep from inability to say anything. It is in this kind of situation that only poetry, which is, in one sense, a convention, but in another sense truer to our inner reality than the miserable words of our everyday speech, can convey anything of the emotion:

Cleopatra: Noblest of men, woo't die?
　　　　　　Hast thou no care of me? shall I abide
　　　　　　In this dull world, which in thy absence is
　　　　　　No better than a sty? O, see, my women,
　　　　　　　　(*Antony dies.*)
　　　　　　The crown o' the earth doth melt.—My lord!
　　　　　　O, wither'd is the garland of the war,
　　　　　　The soldier's pole is faln; young boys and girls
　　　　　　Are level now with men; the odds is gone,
　　　　　　And there is nothing left remarkable
　　　　　　Beneath the visiting moon.
　　　　　　　Antony and Cleopatra, Act IV, Sc. 13

How is a superhuman serenity, a finality never found in real life, to be conveyed in prose? The idea can be suggested in poetry:

Prospero:　　　　　　These our actors,
　　　　　　As I foretold you, were all spirits, and
　　　　　　Are melted into air, into thin air:
　　　　　　And, like the baseless fabric of this vision,
　　　　　　The cloud-capp'd towers, the gorgeous palaces,
　　　　　　The solemn temples, the great globe itself,
　　　　　　Yea, all which it inherit, shall dissolve,

> And, like this unsubstantial pageant faded,
> Leave not a rack behind. We are such stuff
> As dreams are made on; and our little life
> Is rounded with a sleep.
>
> > *The Tempest*, Act IV, Sc. 1

The value of verse for heightening emotion and making violent emotion paradoxically more convincing by placing it within a convention is demonstrated in somewhat extreme form in the 'heroic plays' fashionable in England during the Restoration period, a type of play in which heroes and heroines carried violence of emotion and exaggerations of honour and sentiment far beyond anything in Shakespeare and often far beyond the normal behaviour of people of sound mind. In prose these overstrained emotions would be insufferable, mere embarrassingly impossible melodrama like *George Barnwell*; in verse, in the better plays of this type, it has perhaps a certain flamboyant dignity:

Sebastian: Some strange reverse of fate must sure attend
This vast profusion, this extravagance
Of heven, to bless me thus. 'Tis gold so pure,
It cannot bear the stamp, without allay.
Be kind, ye powers! and take but half away!
With ease the gifts of fortune I resign;
But let my love and friend be ever mine.

> > DRYDEN: *Don Sebastian*, Act IV, Sc. 3

This technique does not always succeed; in the following speech it seems to me that the verse begins well, with a hint of Marlowe, but ends in images that do not fit the context and are somewhat bathetic:

Zara: Yet thus, thus fall'n, thus levell'd with the vilest,
If I have gain'd thy love, 'tis glorious ruin;
Ruin! 'tis still to reign, and to be more
A queen; for what are riches, empire, power,
But larger means to gratify the will?
The steps on which we tread, to rise and reach

133

> Our wish; and that obtain'd, down with the scaffold-
> ing
> Of sceptres, crowns and thrones; they've serv'd their
> end,
> And are, like lumber, to be left and scorn'd.
>
> CONGREVE: The Mourning Bride

An attempt at using verse for the heightening of emotion that does not succeed is Lord Lytton's play *The Lady of Lyons*, comically unreal in diction, though with a good plot in its way; it was very popular when first performed:

Melnotte: Thank Heaven I had no weapon, or I should have slain them. Wretch! What can I say? Where turn? On all sides mockery; the very boors with-in—(*laughter from the Inn*)—'Sdeath, if even in this short absence the exposure should have chanced. I will call her. We will go hence. I have already sent one I can trust to my mother's house. There, at least, none can insult her agony; gloat upon her shame! There alone must she learn what a villain she has sworn to love.

(*As he turns to the door enter Pauline from the Inn.*)

Pauline: Ah! my lord, what a place! I never saw such rude people. I think the very sight of a prince, though he travels *incognito*, turns their honest heads. What a pity the carriage should break down in such a spot! You are not well; the drops stand on your brow; your hand is feverish.

Melnotte: Nay, it is but a passing spasm; the air—

Pauline: Is not the soft air of your native south;
(*Pause*)
How pale he is! indeed thou art not well.
Where are our people? I will call them. (*Going*)

Melnotte: Hold!
I—I am well.

Pauline: Thou art—Ah! now I know it.

Verse and Prose in Drama

> Thou fanciest, my kind lord—I know thou
>   doest—
> Thou fanciest these rude walls, these rustic gos-
>   sips,
> Brick'd floors, sour wine, coarse viands, vex
>   Pauline;
> And so they might, but thou art by my side,
> And I forget all else.

In a number of modern plays a *quotation* from great poetry is used at a crucial moment, since modern practice does not permit the dramatist to drop suddenly into blank verse as Shakespeare would have done. Blake is quoted twice in J. B. Priestley's *Time and the Conways* and fragments of *A Midsummer Night's Dream* in his *Summer Day's Dream*. The passage from *The Tempest*, quoted above, is used in Drinkwater's *Abraham Lincoln*, which also has verse interludes and even such a light and frothy play as Noel Coward's *Present Laughter* uses a passage from Shelley half-tenderly, half-flippantly to underline an emotional crisis. A different kind of evocative quotation is found in T. S. Eliot's *The Cocktail Party*, a play in verse, but verse coming near to conversational language; there a passage from Shelley is used to heighten the emotion at one point.

Verse is also used for some kinds of comic effect, as in the third passage from *The Comedy of Errors* quoted above. A greater exuberance of diction is often possible in verse; today we find this especially in Christopher Fry, whose humour is often as imaginative, inventive and vehement as his passion or enquiry:

> Poor father. In the end he walked
> In Science like the densest night. And yet
> He was greatly gifted.
> When he was born he gave an algebraic
> Cry; at one glance measured the cubic content
> Of that ivory cone his mother's breast
> And multiplied his appetite by five.

Conventions

> So he matured by a progression, gained
> Experience by correlation, expanded
> Into a marriage by contraction, and by
> Certain physical dynamics
> Formulated me. And on he went
> Still deeper into the calculating twilight
> Under the twinkling of five-pointed figures
> Till Truth became for him the sum of sums
> And Death the long division.
>
> *The Lady's Not for Burning*, Act II

In inferior drama the pseudo-poetic is not uncommon; if much of the more pedestrian verse of Shakespeare could have been prose with the mere removal of metre, the verse of many bad plays no longer performed is mere iambic pentameter, formally worked out and without either beauty or rhythm or interesting images—*blank* verse indeed.

Archbishop of Sens:
> Oh, may they never be again laid down,
> Till England is repaid with all the plagues
> Her sons have brought to France! My eager soul,
> As does the fever'd lip for moisture, longs
> To see destruction overwhelm that people.

Ribemont:
> Indulge no guilty hatred, reverend lord;
> For fair report, and, let me add, experience,
> Picture them lovely to impartial judgement.
> The world allows they're valiant, generous, wise,
> Endow'd with all that dignifies our nature!
> While, for their monarch—we'll appeal to facts,
> And sure they speak him wonderful indeed!
>
> W. SHIRLEY: *Edward the Black Prince*[1]

It is harder to write the best prose of Shakespeare, Con-

---

[1] The reader may like to see a note found in my old edition of this play: 'Mr. Shirley, we had almost forgot to mention, intended the play which follows, to resemble the tragedy of Shakespeare.'

greve or Shaw than the blank verse of *Titus Andronicus, The Mourning Bride* or *The Admirable Bashville*, and only the last of these three was intended to be funny. Even the prose of drama is heightened prose. Perhaps often poetic drama, when it is true poetic drama and not merely clumsy formal verse, is written by dramatists who are naturally poets, that is, who include among their gifts a passionate and exceptional delight in language for its own sake, whereas prose drama is written by those who are naturally prose writers, that is, who find language of interest simply as an instrument of communication that for their purposes is fairly satisfactory, though poetry is often trying to communicate the incommunicable. The poetic prose of Flecker or Synge comes somewhere between the two: the mixture of poetry and prose in a Shakespeare or a Dryden[1] is dictated by the operations of genius which can handle poetry or prose equally well, often reducing the distance between the two and using each as it seems more appropriate to the subject matter.

The real motives are probably buried in the bodily rhythms or the subconscious mind; like the whole question of the origin of art, the problem is not capable of full solution; but there are also dramatic conventions of the use of prose and poetry in drama, otherwise there would hardly be so much pseudo-poetic drama forced out by people who were not naturally poets. On the whole it is accepted that in the Elizabethan, Jacobean and 'heroic' drama persons of high rank speak in verse, servants and rustics in prose. In periods when the majority of working people were illiterate and the aristocracy cultivated the arts with enthusiasm, the social differences in speech would be much greater than they are today, and this convention was probably founded on observation. Yet a realistic portrayal of these differences would hardly have been acceptable to the socially very mixed theatre audiences of the period; and it is possible that

[1] Dryden seems to me to have been a real genius who was less lucky in his historical, artistic and intellectual environment than Shakespeare, but I may be quite wrong.

one class could not have understood the idiom of another, as is still true today to a small extent and at the most extreme distances of education or rank. The convention that the more elegant and studied speech and larger vocabulary of the aristocracy should be suggested by verse and common speech by prose was as good a way as any of suggesting class distinctions without insult. (It could be argued that the silliness given to servants on the stage today is more insulting than a mere differentiation of speech!) In some of the ancient Indian drama upper-class people speak Sanskrit and lower-class people Prakrit, another way of giving distinction without degradation, rather as if the King spoke Latin and the pantry-boy colloquial Italian.

This convention is, however, suspended when aristocrats, such as Beatrice and Benedick, are engaged in light trivial talk, or when a servant is showing nobility and magnanimity, like old Adam in *As You Like It*. Another convention that cuts across the class distinctions is that prose is often, very comprehensibly, given to villains, such as Don John in *Much Ado about Nothing*, sometimes Iago in *Othello*, Thersites in *Troilus and Cressida*, or to cynics, such as Lucio in *Measure for Measure* or Pandarus in *Troilus and Cressida*; if such people experience some stronger, worthier or more dignified emotion they may rise to poetry. In *Othello* prose is used for Iago's most base and contemptible speeches, as when he is talking to Roderigo; the 'inner truth' revealed when he is talking to himself is expressed in verse. Enobarbus in *Antony and Cleopatra* makes his cynical speeches in prose but describes Cleopatra's bewitching charms in verse; in his repentance and death after deserting his master he is given particularly eloquent verse. Shylock speaks in prose in business negotiation but in verse in the Trial Scene and at other moments of powerful emotion. In the two *Henry IV* plays, Prince Henry speaks prose with his cronies of the tavern, but verse in any more princely occupation; this distinction is so marked that when a (prose) revel in the tavern is interrupted by the arrival of the Sheriff to enquire about some stolen

Verse and Prose in Drama

property, Prince Henry, leaving his companions, addresses the Sheriff in blank verse. As soon as the Sheriff has gone Prince Henry returns to prose and his low company.

Much can be learned about character and stagecraft by the student who, examining a play by Shakespeare, Dryden or one of the contemporaries of either, stops at every point in the script where there is a change from verse to prose or the reverse, and asks why this change is made. This is perhaps most marked in Shakespeare's later plays, but is worth considering in every play of his in which it occurs, even the introduction of a very small scrap of blank verse in *The Merry Wives of Windsor* having a definite dramatic function. It is also useful to watch the changes from rhyme to blank verse and vice versa; this may have different reasons at different periods. The use of one rhymed couplet to end a scene is simply a convention, but there are other and subtler functions, some conventional, some individual.

The student should incidentally remember that anything called a Song in a play was meant to be sung, and it should thus be considered not just as a piece of poetry in the script but also as a musical effect. In the study of modern drama a consciousness of the problems touched upon here is still useful, whether for considering the limitations of the modern quasi-realistic prose drama, or for studying the immensely difficult problems of diction and a different kind of realism posed by the continuing urge to write modern poetic drama. If we want to extract the last drops of interest out of a script, it is always worth while to make this imaginary journey to the dramatist's study and try to understand what requirements of the stage compelled the use of this or that device or type of diction. This makes many previously incomprehensible things comprehensible and even many faults excusable.

Part Two

STUDY FOR EXAMINATIONS

X. THE TYPES OF DRAMA

'A tedious brief scene of young Pyramus
And his love Thisbe; very tragical mirth.'
Merry and tragical! tedious and brief!
That is, hot ice and wondrous strange snow.
A Midsummer Night's Dream, Act V, Sc.1

ALL definitions in the various fields of art are dangerous, because they are inevitably too narrow somewhere. *King Lear* is probably the most profound and agonizing of Shakespeare's tragedies, yet even in this fragments of the comic are to be found. Even more surprisingly, in the *Antigone* of Sophocles there is a soldier who can be interpreted as a comic character. The 'purest' tragedy I know is that of Racine, which is alien to the tastes of many English people. Similarly, *Much Ado About Nothing* is certainly a comedy; but even the more callous Elizabethans would hardly have found the sight of a young girl fainting at the altar after a false accusation on her wedding day an amusing sight. *Measure for Measure* is a comedy, if a comedy is a play with a happy ending; but its main theme is a cruel and insoluble dilemma treated with passion and pathos. *Volpone* is roaring comedy, but the predicament of the good and modest Celia is not funny, and her speech suggests a serious treatment of that part of the plot:

Celia: O God, and his good angels! whither, whither,
Is shame fled human breasts? that with such ease,
Men dare put off your honours, and their own?
Is that, which ever was a cause of life,
Now placed beneath the basest circumstance,
And modesty an exile made, for money?

Act III, Sc. 6

143

Study for Examinations

Romeo and Juliet is a tragedy, but contains two wonderful comic characters, Mercutio and Juliet's Nurse.

The mixture of tragedy and comedy is, indeed, true to our usual experience of life. In the same small community there may, at the same time, be sickness and a success, a broken engagement and a happy match made, a death and a birth, an absurdly funny incident in the kitchen and a painful interview in the front room. Life is like that. This should surely justify Shakespeare and other writers in mixing the two atmospheres; moreover, there are some people who take life tragically and others shallower but sometimes easier to live with, who take most of it as a comedy; this is a matter of temperament more than experience. Dr. Johnson has said in his Preface to Shakespeare:

'Shakespeare has united the powers of exciting laughter and sorrow not only in one mind, but in one composition. Almost all his plays are divided between serious and ludicrous characters, and, in the successive evolutions of the design, sometimes produce seriousness and sorrow, and sometimes levity and laughter.

'That this is a practice contrary to the rules of criticism will be readily allowed; but there is always an appeal open from criticism to nature. The end of writing is to instruct; the end of poetry is to instruct by pleasing. That the mingled drama may convey all the instruction of tragedy or comedy cannot be denied because it includes both in its alternations of exhibition and approaches nearer than either to the appearance of life, by showing how great machinations and slender designs may promote or obviate one another, and the high and low co-operate in the general system by unavoidable concatenation.'

We may feel nowadays that there is a little too much suet in Dr. Johnson's diction, but we shall hardly wish to dispute the truth of what he has to say.

There may be other mixtures of supposed types besides the mixture of comedy and tragedy. In Jonson and in many of the Restoration dramatists the Comedy of Manners,

The Types of Drama

satirizing current foibles, is often combined with the Comedy of Intrigue. *Richard II* is a historical play, *Henry VIII* a historical play such as could even be reckoned a costume play, but both, with their strong character interest and marked change of fortune, could well be classed as tragedies. For that matter, *Macbeth* could have been classed as a history, for Shakespeare took the subject from Holinshed's *Chronicle*. Priestley's *I Have Been Here Before* is a drama of ideas, in that it discusses a special theory about Time; a comedy, in that it has a happy ending; and even a near-tragedy in that some of the subject-matter is serious and sorrowful. Afinogenov's *Distant Point*—a Soviet play several times produced in England—is a Communist propaganda play, but does not lack a genuine tragic element; Goethe's *Faust* might be called a philosophical tragedy on the most awful theme imaginable, but is also full of comedy, satire, farce and lyrical passages. Examples of the mixture of types could be multiplied almost indefinitely, perhaps more easily among acknowledged masterpieces than among cruder commercial works, which are more apt to fit a formula, having often been composed to one.

However, if this continual overlapping and even contradiction be borne in mind, it is useful to have some rough classification of the kinds of drama; Shakespeare's first publishers evidently felt this when they divided the plays into 'Comedies', 'Histories' and 'Tragedies'. Shakespeare's Polonius, who fancied himself as a critic, though with little justification, was more fastidious in his distinctions, if, like most prigs, less helpful:

'The best actors in the world, either for tragedy, comedy, history, pastoral, pastoral-comical, historical-pastoral, tragical-historical, tragical-comical-historical-pastoral, scene individable, or poem unlimited.'

Hamlet, Act II, Sc. 2

Some further terms are certainly required to classify the whole of the drama that is normally accessible to people

145

in this country, but we will avoid the hyphenations of Polonius.

First we must pay attention to the traditional distinction between tragedy and comedy; this is real and important. The original distinction, usually learned, still, as the school definition, is that tragedy has a sad ending and comedy a happy ending. For dramatic purposes this usually means that tragedy ends with at least one death and comedy with at least one marriage or reconciliation, though in real life death may often be a liberation from suffering and a marriage may sometimes be the beginning of long-drawn-out misery. As in all the classifications of literature, however, the tone of voice, as it were, the general mode of thought, the emotional approach to the subject, is more important than the nature of the end. Aristotle said that tragedy purged our minds by means of pity and terror; Molière implied that the function of comedy was to make decent folk laugh; these definitions are more satisfactory. Tragedy treats life seriously and with a sense of its importance but also of its difficulties; it deals with conflict, dilemma and suffering; comedy is light-hearted and has often a better sense of proportion from the common-sense point of view, but is usually shallower. When a comedy has real depth, as in J. M. Barrie's *Dear Brutus* or Christopher Fry's *The Lady's Not for Burning*, the spectator probably feels a touch of the breath of tragedy.

The diction of tragedy is usually more dignified, and poetic tragedy is much commoner than poetic comedy; the attitude to life and especially to the problems of personal relationships taken in tragedy is more austere and more responsible; there may, as in Greek or Racinian tragedy or the four greatest tragedies of Shakespeare, or the best of Ibsen, be an almost continuous heightening of emotion from beginning to end of the play, whereas in comedy, though there may be tension, it is not continuous and we do not expect anything very serious to happen. A tragedy, even today, may remind us that the earliest function of drama was, so far as we know, magical or religious. A comedy is not likely to do this. Tragedy is more likely to be set among such people as kings, statesmen or at least the rich and cultured, for in tragedy the catastrophe should, to gain its greatest possible force, affect a whole community; in comedy the reactions of six people in a drawing-room may suffice, so the middle classes provide most of the social environments for comedy. One of the effects of the spread of political democracy has been that tragedy now often has working people for its heroes and heroines—this is a valuable broadening of the possibilities of drama. In Sheriff's *Journey's End* ordinary young soldiers in a dug-out are treated tragically; in Eliot's *The Family Reunion* a fairly ordinary family (though it is mildly aristocratic) provides the material for poetic tragedy with a Greek inspiration; in J. M. Synge's *Riders to the Sea* poor peasants have tragic dignity.

The main types of drama may be listed for the use of the student, but with the warning that in all classes there are exceptions, overlaps and anomalies.

1. *Tragedy*

A play with a sorrowful ending, usually at least one death; the action and thoughts are treated seriously and with a respect for human personality. The central character, according to Aristotle—and this still often holds—is a person of admirable character and important position who is ruined by some one flaw of character such as the impetuosity of Oedipus, the ambition of Macbeth or the credulity of Othello. It is usual for the diction to be dignified, but not necessarily poetic or even dignified in the sense of being correct English —the dignity comes from within and expresses the tragic importance of the human beings and their situations, as in the colloquial language of *A Streetcar Named Desire*, parts of *Children in Uniform*, or Arthur Miller's *The Crucible* and *Death of a Salesman*. An important feature of true tragedy is that we are left with a sense of the greatness of man as well as of the suffering involved in human life; these small but passionately individual creatures who struggle with their

147

destiny are curiously important. In tragedy, after one of the crises, the human dilemma becomes insoluble; there is no going back and no easy answer or happy ending; the emotional conflicts are deep and almost unbearable; but the creatures suffering these agonies are worth our concern.

2. *Melodrama*

This is the poor relation of tragedy. It may have a sad or a happy ending, though the sad ending—a pile of corpses or a screaming lunatic—is perhaps more completely melodramatic. It is distinguished from true tragedy by a portrayal of characters who are all more violently and improbably good or evil than is realistic; by a lack of real psychological insight; by a more far-fetched plot whose horrors and sensations may easily tumble over into the ludicrous; and by a continual pandering to the public desire for strong sensations and great excitement. Melodrama may also fall into sentimentality when an attempt is made to portray a tender or lofty emotion. Shakespeare's *Titus Andronicus* and *The Jew of Malta* of Marlowe are two early melodramas, and it does not take much insight to see that these are not plays on the tragic level of *Othello* or *Edward II*.

It is possible, however, to dismiss a play too readily as melodrama. There is good melodrama, now sometimes referred to in catalogues simply as 'drama' or 'strong drama', and bad melodrama. A dreadful example of melodrama which at no point rings true, largely because of the artificiality of its dialogue, is *George Barnwell*, already quoted. Lord Lytton's *The Lady of Lyons* has a most improbable plot and the dialogue is not adequate to the theme, but it is not entirely without merit and might make quite a good play if sincerely performed. (I have not had an opportunity of seeing it.) W. W. Jacobs's *The Monkey's Paw* is an example of intelligent melodrama that is not to be despised, though it might be argued that the theme of wishes being fulfilled in such a way as to bring misery has strong tragic overtones and it is these that give dignity to the play. Quite a number of good modern plays have elements of melodrama but are far from being without literary merit. James Bridie's *Dr. Angelus* and *The Anatomist* both have very sensational plots —but the plot of the second is founded on fact! In each of these plays the characters, or some of them, are richer and more rounded than in the old barn-storming melodrama, and the dialogue is much more lifelike; yet these plays do not reach the heights we usually associate with true tragedy. They might perhaps be given some such name as naturalistic or perhaps journalistic tragedy.

In distinguishing between tragedy and melodrama we should remember that the plot of a great tragedy may be highly sensational—all those of Shakespeare are—but that, unlike the plot of melodrama, it will have a certain air of psychological probability. We should also remember that real life is a good deal more sensational than some of the more cloistered critics have been willing to allow; there is enough of the irrational and violent in ordinary human nature to create a good many sensational plots in a year or so!

3. *The Heroic Play*

This was a type of exaggerated tragedy in vogue in Britain at the time of Dryden. It deals with themes of love and valour and the style is so high-flown as nowadays to seem almost absurd. There may be a surprisingly vulgar and often incongruous sub-plot. The endeavour was presumably to produce something greater than traditional tragedy, and the craving for very strong sensations may have been part of the reaction against Puritanism; but the form is now dead. Examples are Congreve's *The Mourning Bride* and Dryden's *Don Sebastian* and *The Conquest of Granada*. Dryden's *All for Love* may probably be reckoned as a true tragedy.

4. *Problem Play*

This is a useful term to apply to the kind of play which treats of a particular social or moral problem so as to make people think intelligently about it. It is usually somewhat tragic in tone in that it naturally deals with painful human dilemmas; it is the kind of play that, by implication, asks a definite question and either supplies an answer or leaves it to us to find one. It is a popular mode of drama of the late nineteenth century and the twentieth century; but *Measure for Measure* and perhaps *Hamlet* could be placed in this category, and several of the Greek plays, such as *Antigone*, *Electra* and *Choephoroe*, could be taken as such, though they would not so have been taken by their original audiences, since the familiar myth then dictated the only solution of the problem.

Most of the plays of Ibsen and Shaw are problem plays; other modern examples are Clemence Dane's *A Bill of Divorcement*, dealing with problems of divorce and heredity and incidentally showing very cleverly how the most tragic human problems may be further complicated by other people's lack of comprehension; Somerset Maugham's *The Sacred Flame*, in which a mother kills her son for reasons which many people might call adequate; J. B. Priestley's *Home is Tomorrow*, whose theme is more elusive but might perhaps be called 'what is civilization and what are its important values?'; Peggy Barnwell's *Prison Without Bars* and Elsa Shelley's *Pick-Up Girl* on themes of juvenile delinquency; Emlyn Williams's *The Corn is Green* on education and the difficulties in its way; Terence Rattigan's *The Winslow Boy* on the question of the relative importance of State and individual; and several recent plays of very varied quality on the subject of nuclear weapons. The problem play is very popular today and is likely to be popular in any period when ideas are changing and society is developing rapidly. It is a type of play that appeals to vigorous, thoughtful minds and can thus make a small contribution to human progress; but it is apt to over-simplify problems for the sake of dramatic effect and it may be over-melodramatic.

5. Comedy

The essential function of tragedy is to make people think

The Types of Drama

and feel more deeply; the essential function of comedy is to amuse. The amusement may range from a quiet smile to a guffaw. Comedy can be very sophisticated or very simple; it can also be warm-hearted and human, like Eden Philpotts's *Yellow Sands* and *The Farmer's Wife*, or brilliant but heartless, like *The Provok'd Wife* or *The Way of the World*. Comedy may usefully be subdivided into the types that follow.

6. *Comedy of Errors*[1]

There is a type of comedy in which the plot consists of a series of mistakes of identity or fact, or misinterpretations of action or character, resulting in much talk at cross-purposes. It is almost one of the recognized conventions of drama that such mistakes shall be made more easily in drama than in real life, so that husbands and wives, parents and children, pairs of friends and of sweethearts, shall fail to recognize each other because of some disguise perhaps as simple as a mask or boy's clothes on a girl and vice versa. On the stage we have very little difficulty in accepting this. Shakespeare's *Comedy of Errors* is an obvious example of this type; his *Twelfth Night* is probably the best of the kind ever written; and Goldsmith's *She Stoops to Conquer* is another masterpiece in the genre.

7. *Comedy of Manners*

This is comedy in which the amusement arises mostly from the portrayal of current foibles or minor social abuses, or recognized social 'types' such as the vulgar *nouveau-riche*, the climber, the gossip, the snob and so on. The characterization may be more or less rich, the plot more or less interesting; but the chief pleasure in the language and habits portrayed. Examples are Shakespeare's *Love's Labour's Lost*, Molière's *Les Femmes Savantes* and *Les Précieuses Ridicules*, Jonson's *Bartholomew Fair*, Sheridan's *The School for Scandal*

[1] This is my own title and it might be wiser not to use it in an examination.

Study for Examinations

and *The Critic*, Etherege's *The Man of Mode*, Congreve's *The Old Bachelor*, Farquhar's *The Recruiting Officer*, to some extent Barrie's *Alice Sit-by-the Fire*. Steele's *The Conscious Lovers* is a warmer Comedy of Manners in which an attempt is made not only to satirize current foibles but to suggest better modes of behaviour. Steele's *The Tender Husband* is another play of this kind. The last two plays overlap into the next category.

8. *Sentimental Comedy*

As its name implies, this is comedy which seeks to play to some extent upon our sympathies as well as making us laugh; it may even draw easy tears. It was, historically, a reaction against the coarseness and heartlessness of the brilliant but usually scandalous Restoration Comedy; but the genre is certainly far from extinct. Steele furnishes some of the best examples; other examples are Hugh Kelly's *A Word to the Wise*, which is more sentimental and less comic, and Isaac Bickerstaff's *The Maid of the Mill* and *Love in a Village*, two pretty comedies of excellent moral tone by an author whose character is said to have been scandalous! A modern example of some merit is Dodie Smith's *Dear Octopus*; Hollywood at its worst will provide abundant examples of this genre at its lowest.

9. *Comedy of Character or Humours*

Here the chief comic interest is in the characters themselves —which is rather deeper and more difficult to convey than mere mannerisms and foibles. All Shakespeare's comedies are more or less comedies of character, just as they are all more or less comedies of errors. Jonson specialized in the comedy of humours, which is a kind of simplified comedy of character taking one point as characteristic to each person, so that we can have a jealous man, an ill-tempered man, a generous man, a lazy man and so on, but little complexity; this method was based on early physiological and psychological theories now known to be incorrect—though they

The Types of Drama

were not stupid in their time. Whereas in tragedy we see people suffering because of their characters, in comedy we see them make fools of themselves because of their reactions to the comic situations; destiny in comedy brings out the humorous side of character. The treatment of character in comedy may range from the cynical and almost contemptuous, as in Jonson's *The Silent Woman* or Somerset Maugham's *The Breadwinner*, to the kindly and affectionate treatment of human fallibility as in *As You Like It*, Noel Coward's *The Young Idea* and Christopher Fry's *Venus Observed*. Sometimes in the comedy of character it is only the principal character who is really comic; for instance, in Molière's *L'Avare* only the miser Harpagon is really comic; the other characters, especially the young lovers, give the impression of being quite reasonable beings. Or, as in Jonson's comedies, all the characters may be comic. A good comedy of errors such as *She Stoops to Conquer* also has a strong character-interest.

10. Farce

Farce is to comedy roughly what melodrama is to tragedy —it aims at producing laughter by exaggerated effects of various kinds and is without psychological depth. Characterization and wit are less important than a rapid succession of amusing situations. The comic situations are generally rather crude; farce has been called 'custard-pie comedy' because it often uses such purely material absurdities as people throwing custard pies or other messy things at each other's heads, heavy falls or instances of the perversity of inanimate objects. Surprises, coincidences and exaggerations abound. Probability is not much regarded. The form is on a relatively low artistic level, but good farce, like good melodrama, may show a high standard of craftsmanship in the writing, and it demands a high standard of slick production, especially in timing. Good farce is usually nearer to the comedy of errors than to the other kinds of comedy. Such old plays as *Gammer Gurton's Needle* and *Thersites* (in

153

which a boaster is afraid of a snail) might be said to be farces—very good ones—but it would be more accurate historically to class them as primitive comedies. Farces of some merit in the craftsmanship are Brandon Thomas's *Charley's Aunt*, which has enjoyed popularity since 1892, Garrick's *Miss in her Teens* and Colman's *The Deuce is in Him*, both of which are still successful on the stage in slightly modernized versions, although they were written in the eighteenth century; Terence Rattigan's *French Without Tears*, and Sean O'Casey's *The End of the Beginning* are among the numerous good twentieth-century farces.

11. *The Drama of Ideas*

It could be argued that there is no real distinction between the drama of ideas and the problem play or propaganda play; but I think there is a separate type of drama in which the pleasure and interest are almost entirely intellectual and our emotions are not as much affected as they are by both tragedy and comedy. The excitement of such a play lies in the play of ideas and the interest of speculation; it sets people talking and puts various points of view, some of them unusual. The problems implied are not such as we generally try to solve; no solution need be implied; but we like to think about the issues raised. Shaw's *Back to Methuselah*, *Man and Superman* and *The Apple Cart* are examples of the drama of ideas, whereas *Widowers' Houses* and *Mrs. Warren's Profession* are true problem plays in which we are expected to want to improve a stated situation. Somerset Maugham's *Sheppey*, in which a man suddenly becomes rich and interprets Christianity in a more literal way than usual, is probably mostly a drama of ideas; *The Circle* has some of this kind of interest, though it is that rather unsatisfactory form, a light-comedy treatment of a theme that is tragic or nearly so. A lesser but ingenious example of the drama of ideas is Sutton Vane's *Outward Bound*. The form, like the problem play, is popular in an age of shifting values; early examples are difficult to find; but it could be said that there

were considerable elements of the drama of ideas in Shakespeare's *Coriolanus* and *Troilus and Cressida* and in Marlowe's *Dr. Faustus*.

12. *Didactic Drama—Propaganda Plays*

The use of the theatre for direct propaganda is actually
nothing new; all the Miracle and Morality plays of Britain
and Europe were instructional dramas explaining the doc-
trines of the Church; but nowadays we are more self-conscious about a propaganda element in a play, because the
drama has long escaped from the need for a religious justification and there is much drama that is not propagandist.[1]
The propaganda play or didactic drama is one in which the
primary motive of the play is the impressing of an idea on an
audience, generally a religious, political or social idea. It is,
of course, impossible for an intelligent person to write plays
for long without at some time expressing or implying a view
on some important issue. Shakespeare is full of the political
theories natural to his epoch, and sometimes, as in *King
Lear*, of ideas ahead of his time; but even in *Henry V* he is
not really a writer of propaganda plays.

Examples of the true propaganda play are Priestley's *They
Came to a City* (creative humanitarian socialism) and *Cornelius* (the sterility of capitalism); Clifford Odets's *Waiting
for Lefty* (workers' solidarity); Galsworthy's *Justice* (the
complete inadequacy of legal justice—a play which contributed a good deal to prison reform); Auden and Isherwood's *The Dog Beneath the Skin* (the degeneracy of capi-
talist society), Christa Winsloe's *Children in Uniform* (against
repressive education and unnatural segregation); Dorothy
Sayers's *The Man Born to be King* (dramatic restatement of
the Gospel story); and a great many plays performed at
church festivals. It should not be assumed that the didactic
play is necessarily a bad play; there have been some very
bad ones, but all those mentioned above have some literary

[1] 'Escapist' literature, even, is propaganda for 'not bothering'—and
can sometimes be dangerous as such!

155

merit. It can however, seldom be a supremely great play, as for the sake of the propaganda it must over-simplify and probably overstate.

The rise of Communism has contributed to the rise of didactic drama as a serious art form; in Russia the theatre has been treated as an important instrument of public education for Communism, and this movement has produced such good and human dramas as Afinogenev's *Distant Point*, as well as a good deal of naïve and over-simplified drama of no literary value. The theatre in China is now being used in the same way and, again, not all the plays produced are without literary merit. Many plays are written for schools with the intention of conveying necessary information in a palatable form; and Schools Broadcasts dramatize history or geography or biography to make it more memorable. Most of these are of small literary value but educationally excellent.

13. *The History Play—the Episodic Play*

The division of Shakespeare's plays into Tragedies, Comedies and Histories is a real division, though we do not now speak as readily of the History as of the other two forms. History naturally provides a great deal of dramatic material. (Biography may be regarded as an aspect of history.) There can be true tragedies based on history, such as Shakespeare's *Julius Caesar*, *Coriolanus* and *Antony and Cleopatra*; Jonson's *Sejanus* and *Catiline*; Ford's *Perkin Warbeck*; Dryden's *All for Love*; Rostand's *L'Aiglon*. There can also be true comedy based on history, though this is less usual, in that the surviving records of humanity are mostly of the serious episodes. Examples of historical comedy are Shaw's *In Good King Charles' Golden Days*, R. E. Sherwood's *The March to Rome* and several of Maurice Baring's *Diminutive Dramas*. A theme from history may be chosen for the light it seems to throw on some topical problem, as in a number of Soviet films. Queen Elizabeth I even felt that *Richard II* was dangerously topical. This method has often been used to comment upon current events in totalitarian countries, without bringing disaster upon the writer. Conversely a historical theme may be chosen because it is sufficiently removed from the topical to give opportunities for heightened emotion, universality, poetic language or pageantry; a historical play in which the glamour rather than the general truth and reality of history is the attraction is often known to producers as a costume play; the cast can enjoy dressing up in pretty clothes and any lack of conviction will with luck be attributed to the different period. A good many plays dealing with Jacobite episodes or with the Tudor period are no more than costume plays, and both these themes need a rest.

Thus any kind of drama, even farce, can have a theme from history as its source. There is however a separate type of historical drama which is different in construction from other plays—Shakespeare's Histories fall into this category. The unity necessary to a play is found in the logical sequence of a succession of episodes rather than in the Aristotelian unities. There may be a marked mixture of tragic and comic episodes, aimed at giving a representation of life as it is; several themes may be interwoven; and the action extends over a long period of time, a lifetime or even more. Another name sometimes used for this type of play is the Chronicle Play. Shakespeare's *Henry IV* (both parts) exemplifies the type; Hardy's *The Dynasts* is an example that is not very successful on the stage, though I believe it succeeds as a radio play. Such plays aim at being representative cross-sections of life in a period. It is also possible to have an episodic play dealing with something less important than history in its usual sense; examples are Arnold Bennett's *Milestones* and Noel Coward's *This Happy Breed*, both dealing with the changing fortunes and experiences of a family; Shakespeare's *Pericles* and Barrie's *Mary Rose*, in which the personal drama is what is important, but the action spreads over a long time; and *The Dog Beneath the Skin* and Anne Ridler's *Henry Bly* in which the adventures, more or less symbolic, of one person link together a series of episodes.

Study for Examinations

Under this heading we may put the *Documentary* play and the *Living Newspaper*, educational or propaganda plays (and, especially, films) which explain something by means of a series of short representative scenes. Many Schools Broadcasts are good examples of this; the Federal Theatre organization in America, which came to an end in 1939, produced many such plays, for example Sidney Howard's *Yellow Jack*, on the fight against yellow fever.

14. *Tragi-Comedy*

It is perhaps desirable that a separate section be given to the play that is so much a mixture of tragic and comic elements as to be called tragi-comedy, though the tendency of all dramatic 'types' to overlap has already been stressed. The mixture of tragic and comic can be very infelicitous, as in Thomas Otway's *Venice Preserved*, in which the total effect of the play is tragic, and, indeed, it is a fairly good tragedy, but there are two comic episodes showing the courtship of a foolish senator and his harsh lady, episodes which are quite out of keeping with the tone of the rest of the play, though in a Restoration comedy they might be quite pleasing. Southern's *Isabella, or The Fatal Marriage* is another play in which the mixture of comic elements rather weakens the effect of the tragic plot, which is a good one.

However, the mixture can be successful, for the reasons already expressed by Dr. Johnson; life is more a tragi-comedy, for most people, than either a tragedy or a comedy. Modern drama, indeed, with its stress on realism, makes much use of the mixed type; many of the plays of Bridie have tragic and comic elements mixed, and usually give the impression of being very lifelike. *The Anatomist* is one possible example. Priestley's *Summer Day's Dream* is mostly a comedy, but has tragic possibilities and at least one character, the Russian visitor, is a tragic figure at the end of the play. T. S. Eliot classed his *The Cocktail Party* as a comedy, and it certainly has much of the tone of comedy throughout; but one of its characters, Celia, the heroine in so far as there

158

is one, suffers a horrible form of martyrdom, which is not exactly a comic theme. Similarly, there are aspects of the Comedy of Manners in Eliot's tragedy, *The Family Reunion*. Almost all Shakespeare's plays are mixed to some degree. The term tragi-comedy may also be applied to plays which have a serious theme but a happy ending, such as *Measure for Measure*.

15. *Symbolic Drama—Expressionism*

There is a form of drama, which can be more truly dramatic than it sounds, in which the characters are not human beings in the ordinary sense, but personifications of single concepts or human characteristics. Expressionism seeks to represent the inner life of human beings by various symbols and special conventions. The limitations of this form are obvious; but it can be moving. The early Morality plays, of which the greatest is *Everyman*, in which a representative human being encounters Death, Knowledge, Confession, Good Deeds and other abstractions, are plays of this kind. *Everyman*, sincerely produced, is very moving, for much of it is of universal appeal. These early plays were rather naïve but can still appeal by their directness and sincerity.

Modern Expressionism is more violently experimental and draws upon the idea of the subconscious and, often, upon the use of associative rather than directly communicative language. A modern British example of some merit is Tyrone Guthrie's *Top of the Ladder*, in which a dying man's mental pictures of his past life are dramatized in language full of significant puns and associations. The form flourished most notably in Germany after the 1914–18 war and before the success of Nazism in nearly obliterating real culture for a time: Ernst Toller (*Masse-Mensch*) and Frank Wedekind (pre-1914—*Frühlings Erwachen*, *Hidalla* and other plays on violent sex themes) have the most obviously permanent reputation in this group. There are Expressionist elements in the work of Čapek and all the poetic plays of W. B. Yeats are more or less symbolical, *The Herne's Egg* being the most difficult and symbolic of these. Symbolic elements now enter into many modern plays.

In this type of drama, scenery, incidental music, special costume, sometimes masks, special lighting effects and other devices of production that are not literary in the ordinary sense may play a vitally important part.

16. *Dance Drama*

There is a pure dance drama that is related to ballet rather than to normal drama as we understand it for the purposes of this book; that is, it is not really a *literary* form, words playing a very small part in it. However, there are literary plays in which dancing plays an important part, for examples, Yeats's *Four Plays for Dancers* (*The Only Jealousy of Emer*, *At the Hawk's Well*, *The Dreaming of the Bones* and *Calvary*). Many of the plays of Rabindranath Tagore, which have been translated into English, use dance as part of the vital action. His very beautiful and simple *Natir Puja* is a play in which—as is generally true of Indian ballet—the function of dance as a form of religious ritual and sacrifice is shown. The Nō plays of Japan (imitated by Yeats) originated in ritual dances and dance is still important in them; dance-drama is very important in the Javanese, Chinese, and Malayan theatres; and the student should remember that most great world drama has arisen from religious rituals, so that there is always a possibility of another great drama developing from a primitive and ritual form.

17. *Mime*

This should be mentioned for the sake of completeness, though less important as a serious art form in England than in France. Mime is silent acting, and there are roughly two branches of the art, the 'classical' mime with a set of recognized characters found in the Italian *commedia dell' arte*, which also used improvised words and in the French and English *harlequinade*; and the 'realistic mime' which has a wider scope and is exemplified in such plays as Thornton

The Types of Drama

Wilder's *The Happy Journey* and *The Long Christmas Dinner*, in which the actors perform with imaginary properties. The form, which demands intense concentration from both actors and audience, has possibilities which have not yet been much explored in England. The French *L'enfant Prodigue* is a full-length mime play. True modern mime is a completely silent art and therefore cannot well be classed as literature. It is very valuable indeed in the educational and psychological field and its use in this field is growing; I can myself testify abundantly to its value in cultivating poise, imagination and dramatic ability among children and students. There is an obvious overlap of Mime and pure Ballet which I am not qualified to discuss.

Pantomime is etymologically and historically related to Mime, but nowdays, in this country, is a spectacular variety show based, often very slenderly, on a nursery-tale and providing a series of pretty, sentimental or vulgar episodes to entertain a Christmas-holiday public.

It would also be possible to classify plays by the way in which language is used. It is certainly desirable that the student of drama should think about the function of language in each play studied. A tentative classification along these lines may be offered here.

1. *True Poetic*

A great heightening of language for dramatic effect, using standard metrical patterns and much imagery. Examples: *Antony and Cleopatra*, *Othello*, Fry's *The Firstborn*, Eliot's *The Family Reunion*, Anne Ridler's *Cain*.

2. *Conventionally Poetic*

Using metrical language because it is the thing to do at the time, when the play, as far as its emotional content goes, could have been written as well in prose, or, sometimes, would have been better not written at all, because no language the writer is capable of using will make it convincing.

161

Study for Examinations

Examples are Shakespeare's *The Comedy of Errors* and Congreve's *The Mourning Bride* as good verse dramas that are not really poetic; Johnson's *Irene* and Rowe's *The Royal Convert* as plays that do not succeed. There are dozens of examples among the obscurer contemporaries of Shakespeare and the obscurer 'heroic' dramatists.

3. *Realistic*

Using language that is meant to give the impression of conversations in real life, though in fact it will always be somewhat heightened and enlivened. This will always be prose drama. Examples may be taken from any of the plays of Shaw, Somerset Maugham, J. M. Barrie, John Galsworthy, J. B. Priestley, Terence Rattigan, Noel Coward and most of the ordinary commercial dramatists. It must be remembered that language which now seems very artificial may have been an attempt at representing the natural diction of the time, as in the plays of Pinero and Henry Arthur Jones, or, probably, Restoration comedy.

4. *Rhetorical*

This word, in a very specialized sense, could be applied to those plays in which much of the delight is in language itself. It seems likely that much of the comedy of the Shakespearian period was strongly influenced by that study of rhetoric which was one of the interests stimulated by the Renaissance; and since then there have been many plays in which the art of elaborate language gave much of the pleasure. Examples are *Love's Labour's Lost*—perhaps the most extreme example of this genre available—*The Taming of the Shrew*, all the plays of Wilde, to some extent those of Christopher Fry, Synge's *The Playboy of the Western World* and, up to a point, Shaw's *Pygmalion*.

5. *Symbolic*

There are a few plays, and there may be more as the drama embarks on new adventures, in which language is used more

The Types of Drama

experimentally and with delicate ambiguities, persistent images or incantatory effects. Hints of this are found as early as Shakespeare, especially in the four great tragedies; modern examples include Eugene O'Neill's *Strange Interlude*, W. B. Yeats's *The Shadowy Waters* and *The Herne's Egg* and Louis MacNeice's *Out of the Picture*.

This classification by language is itself experimental and should be used as a stimulus to thought, not for examination purposes.

The student who desires a wide knowledge of drama should not forget that the RADIO SCRIPT and the FILM SCENARIO are forms of drama. Radio scripts that are easily accessible in book form are Louis MacNeice's *The Dark Tower* and *Christopher Columbus*; very few film scenarios are available to the public as books, but Dylan Thomas's *The Doctor and the Devils* (on the same theme as Bridie's *The Anatomist*, and providing an interesting contrast) is available as a book. His *Under Milk Wood* has enjoyed great success as a radio play and even as a televised or staged drama—a purpose for which it was not intended. Noel Coward's *Still Life* is the germ of the film *Brief Encounter*. It is often worth while to compare a stage play and the film that has been made of it.

XI. RELATING DRAMA TO
HISTORY

Sweet it may be and decorous, perhaps, for the country to die; but,
On the whole we conclude the Romans won't do it, and I shan't.
                    ARTHUR HUGH CLOUGH: *Amours de Voyage*

ALL drama has to be contemporary in its immediate
appeal. It is possible for a Wordsworth, Blake, Keats
to be ridiculed or ignored in his own time, so long
as his books are published, and for him to win a later reputation not likely ever to be destroyed. It is possible for
Thomas Traherne, Christopher Smart and Gerard Manley
Hopkins to become known as minor geniuses only many
years after they wrote. Something similar has very often
happened in the fields of painting and sculpture and could
happen to a novelist. But a dramatist cannot choose to write
for posterity, because his work must be produced on a stage
and he cannot know what the theatre will be like, physically
or spiritually, after a few generations. Shakespeare could
not have anticipated our modern use of such subtle lighting
effects as dimmers, floods, spots and coloured lights, nor the
mechanical devices possible on the modern stage; had such
techniques been available to him he would probably have
been delighted with them and have used them freely to provide exciting supernatural effects and changes of weather.
He could not even anticipate the seemingly more obvious
use of a curtain. Sophocles wrote not for the almost intimate modern theatre but for a huge open-air theatre in
which details of gesture were lost and the actors wore masks.
The Restoration comedy writers did not know that one day
there would be a censorship of the stage. A dramatist must

be produced in order to be known at all, and must therefore write for the available stage techniques. He must please the audience of his own times at least sufficiently to induce them to come to see his plays. The dramatist of today has probably more choice than ever before in the matter of stage organization, though he is limited severely by the number of themes that are already exhausted, by the effects of commercialism and by the censorship.

It does not matter if the dramatist displeases some of his contemporaries; if he has anything at all to say he can hardly help displeasing some of them; and if he has nothing to say he will displease all those who think he ought to have something. He may often be disappointed at the timidity and narrowness even of people who are supposed to be educated, by the intellectual dishonesty that prefers sentimentality to probability, by the star-cult that often makes it advisable to write with a particular actor in mind; by the fact that farce can hope for a long run and a rich reward whereas a fine poetic drama may be produced only in a little theatre for a short time; but he must find *some* audience sufficient to enable a theatre manager to produce his play without ruin; and that audience must consist of his own contemporaries. Even in the Elizabethan period there were both public playhouses with a very mixed audience and so-called 'private' theatres (which produced plays by such people as John Lyly, the Euphuist) and court performances catering for a more refined audience.

When we read a play, especially an old play, we must bear this in mind. Every play that is capable of being performed was written for a specific type of theatre which may not be the one we know. There is an unfortunate tendency among teachers and scholars to look upon actual dramatic productions and the study of the live stage as a 'frill', a luxury; but any study of drama that is not related to the study of the stage is unreal. The reader of Shakespeare must know something about the Elizabethan theatre; he must realize that the banal couplets with which people walk off the stage were an old form of 'curtain'; that certain scenes took place on the balcony or in the 'inner room'; that the stage was very close to the audience; that performances took place in daylight and therefore the time of day or state of the weather had to be described in words; that the costumes worn were not historically accurate but were sumptuous contemporary costume ('Cut my lace, Charmian!' says Cleopatra!); and that there was no scenery in our sense of the word. The student of the Restoration and the eighteenth-century drama should know something about the increasing use of the theatre socially, as a meeting-place; the student of the Greek drama should see a Greek or Roman open-air theatre (the nearest are in France) or, failing that, photographs of one, and should know something about the civic and religious dignity of the Greek drama. The student of drama in 2160 will probably have to spend some time studying the 'primitive twentieth-century stage' and its limitations. In judging a drama we must take into account the limitations of the stage for which it was written; and in making a detailed study of a play we should also bear in mind the intended methods of production.

The dramatist is also limited by contemporary ideas, even apart from censorships and special legal restrictions. He can never be very far ahead of his time in politics, religion, morality, scientific speculation or any other subject on which opinions change. Even in his characterization he is restricted by current assumptions. Aristotle thought that it was not proper for a woman to be represented as clever, a natural enough assumption in a society in which women were subordinate. The women of Shakespeare, who wrote under Queen Elizabeth I in an age in which upper-class women, at least, had some will of their own and could attain some standard of education, can have the lively minds and strong characters of Portia, Rosalind, Beatrice, Imogen, the dignity and courage of Hermione or the education and adaptability of Helena or Marina. They may even have the revolutionary moral courage of the Duchess of Malfi in

Webster's play. But at this period it is still a current assumption that women exist only for marriage, or, more rarely, the religious life, and all these noble women show their strength of character in a context of love. In the twentieth century, when it is recognized that an able woman can make a success of a career and be valuable to society in other contexts than marriage, Shaw can portray Saint Joan, a soldier woman who is indifferent to love, Lina Szczepanowska, the acrobat who is under an obligation to risk her life every day, in *Misalliance*, Vivie Warren the independent woman lawyer in *Mrs. Warren's Profession*, Lavinia the Christian martyr in *Androcles and the Lion* and Lysistrata the woman Cabinet Minister in *The Apple Cart*—dignified and intelligent women who practise professions with success and are willing to die, if need be, not for love but for integrity. Shaw seems to have underrated love as a force in life and a worth-while experience, and love is still one of the great themes of drama as of life; but it is no longer the only possible preoccupation for a woman in drama.

The attitude to power has also changed a great deal. To give a full account of the developments in the attitude to power would involve a study of political philosophy; but we can see it in the Greek dramatists and in Shakespeare as compared with later writers. Shakespeare's Henry V is a model king we are intended to admire; as a young prince he had sown a plentiful crop of wild oats, not from understandable human weakness and curiosity but with the deliberate intention of winning admiration by a spectacular reform; nowadays this, especially with the harsh rejection of his old associates, would be regarded as a contemptible publicity stunt; Henry condemns three traitors to death without trial; he shows himself prepared to carry out a barbarous sack of Harfleur; he frequently boasts of his country in a manner we should now feel was unseemly; and, after a war we should now call aggressive, he imposes a severe peace on France. Anyone who today wrote a play glorifying such acts would run the risk of being called a Fascist; we have seen too much

Study for Examinations

of the evil results of the uncritical glorification of the 'man of action'. But disapproval of 'aggression' is a comparatively modern thing, a mark of advancing civilization and the sense that there is an international law above power.

This does not mean that Shakespeare loved war or had a Nazi-like adoration of power; the man who wrote this:

> And as our vineyards, fallows, meads and hedges,
> Defective in their natures, grow to wildness,
> Even so our houses, and ourselves and children,
> Have lost, or do not learn for want of time,
> The sciences that should become our country;
> But grow, like savages,—as soldiers will,
> That nothing do but meditate on blood,—
> To swearing, and stern looks, diffused attire,
> And everything that seems unnatural.
>
> *Henry V*, Act V, Sc. 2

was aware of the spiritual as well as the material ravages of war; the man who wrote this:

> Merciful Heav'n!
> Thou rather with thy sharp and sulphurous bolt
> Splitt'st the unwedgeable and gnarled oak
> Than the soft myrtle; but man, proud man,
> Drest in a little brief authority,—
> Most ignorant of what he's most assured,
> His glassy essence,—like an angry ape,
> Plays such fantastic tricks before high heaven
> As make the angels weep; who, with our spleens,
> Would all themselves laugh mortal.
>
> *Measure for Measure*, Act II, Sc. 2

was no uncritical respecter of persons and well knew that authority was not restricted to people who could be trusted with it. But Shakespeare's 'good' or 'bad' kings or statesmen must be seen in relationship to his age, in which arbitrary power was more acceptable and war taken more for granted than today.

Relating Drama to History

Whenever we are puzzled by something in an old play that seems to be not simply poor craftsmanship but downright improbable or repulsive, we should find out something about the customs of the period. Judging by *King Lear* and *Timon of Athens* Shakespeare was far from being in perfect and complacent harmony with his age, but the time for the problem play or protest play had not yet come, and he had to write what his contemporaries could understand. We shall often find him more humane and, as it were, more charitably uncertain of many things than most of his contemporaries; that is one reason, though not the most important, why everything he wrote still survives.

The literary standards of a period must also be considered when we examine a play. We must remember that every art goes through a period of infancy and adolescence before it becomes mature. The technical stagecraft of Terence Rattigan is better not only than that of the Miracle Plays but than most of Shakespeare; but Mr. Rattigan's excellent stagecraft and economy were learned from all that had gone before. Drama, with its severe limitations and the need for extreme concentration, is an exacting craft, and it is not surprising that even in the tremendous Elizabethan age with its miracles of poetry and vitality the drama was still feeling its way in the matter of technical craftsmanship. The stage itself was far from ideal—and the ideal stage has not yet been invented. If Sackville's *Gorboduc*, generally treated as the first English tragedy, is well nigh unreadable, it is not because Sackville was a bad writer; his Induction to *The Mirror for Magistrates* proves that he was a poet of considerable merit; but he had no real English tragedies to examine, nothing to help him except some Greek and Latin dramatic criticism written for other ages, and no experience of seeing a good play. Shakespeare's early plays have glaring faults; but they are better than anything he could ever have seen, which is, if we reflect on how much we learn by imitation, outstanding proof of his rare genius. As soon as the wave of interest in drama was swelling, intending dramatists had something to

169

look at, something to argue about, someone to argue with, all of which makes the task of a writer far easier.

Similarly, there was a long period of stagnation in the true stage drama in the nineteenth century; but as soon as a few self-respecting dramatists again appeared—Henry Arthur Jones, Pinero, Wilde, Granville-Barker and the young Shaw —there was again a climate for drama and more dramatists appeared; the standard rose quickly. Shelley's *The Cenci* is not a good stage play, but when we consider that it was written by a man who had practically no opportunity to see worth while new drama it seems a miracle of his genius. William Archer in *The Old Drama and the New* (1923), points out the great faults of craftsmanship in the Elizabethan and Restoration dramatists and compares them unfavourably with the moderns. The book is salutary reading, as is anything that destroys unthinking idolatories; but Archer forgets that the moderns are standing on the shoulders of the ancients and would be blameworthy if they had not learned much about stagecraft—not necessarily about inspiration—from the mistakes of their predecessors. The amazing thing about the early dramatists is not that they sometimes perpetrated wild improbabilities, clumsy devices, pedestrian dialogue and other unworthinesses, but that they wrote so much that was first-rate by any standards.

The standards of factual accuracy and scholarship in drama are probably higher today than they have ever been. The methods of modern historical research and the standards of modern scholarship were quite unknown to the Elizabethans and perhaps may be said to have begun only in the eighteenth century. Anachronisms such as the clock and the dressing-gown (called a nightgown) in *Julius Caesar* or the complete unreality of the Romans and Britons historically in *Cymbeline* should not be judged by the standards applied to a modern historical play or film. All concern for truth is good; our raised standards of scholarship are part of the more fastidious standards of our civilization; but Shakespeare was concerned, not with dramatizing history for a Schools Broadcast, but with the process of extracting drama from history as he knew it.

Much of the earlier drama contains jokes and allusions that we nowadays find offensive—they have usually been cut out of school editions—and the common belief that literature has degenerated in the matter of decency and morality is farcically funny to a serious student of literature; but nothing changes faster than fashions of what is allowable in decent speech, and perhaps I may be allowed to quote Mrs. Slipslop's famous 'Marry-come-up! some people's ears are the nicest part about them!'[1] for the prudes. If we find a joke objectionable it can usually be left out in production. The comedies of the Restoration period are often regarded as unfit for school use, being licentious and often cynical; but if we are tempted to condemn them in spite of their artistic brilliance we should remember that they were written just after the country had been released from a Puritan dictatorship, and that most of us are at our worst just after we have had to be on our unnaturally best behaviour.

Thus all plays need to be seen in relation to their historical background—the theatre of the time, the artistic standards of the time and the general mental and moral climate of the time. We should not cultivate fastidiousness until we become stupid perfectionists like the classicist critic Rymer, who in the eighteenth century called *Othello* 'a bloody farce without salt or savour'! In general we learn far more about a work by approaching it in a spirit of respectful curiosity than by an attitude of resolute destructiveness. We shall always do better in criticism (and, incidentally, be much pleasanter people) if we refrain from assuming that there are some absolute standards for all times and all circumstances; perhaps somewhere in heaven there are absolute standards of art, as the Standard Measures are kept at Greenwich; but how are we, finite, limited, fallible, short-lived creatures that we are, to know them?

A last caution is desirable. It is very easy to adopt a

[1] Fielding: *Joseph Andrews.*

171

patronizing attitude to some branch of art as soon as we have to admit that it has some weaknesses to be excused. I hope I have not seemed to do this myself. We can easily slip into the attitude of admitting that there are faults in Shakespeare's plays, and defending him with the kind of magnanimity which suggests that we, of course, could throw off half a dozen better plays before breakfast. It is always wise to remember that few critics, and this includes not only schoolchildren and students, but paid professional critics, have ever written a good play, and no one has yet written a play accepted by common consent as being better than Shakespeare. It is very much easier to point out how something could have been done better than to do it in any fashion at all. Many people who cannot cook grumble at bad food. The quickest way to acquire a little wholesome respect for the artist who, however fallible, is creative, is to do a charade or, better, to write a simple one-act play or scene from a projected play. In approaching literature as in judging persons, we should always avoid the merely destructive attitude, from which we learn nothing.

XII. THE USELESSNESS AND USE OF NOTES

The art of writing notes is not of difficult attainment. The work is performed, first by railing at the stupidity, negligence, ignorance and asinine tastelessness of the former editors, and shewing, from all that goes before and all that follows, the inelegance and absurdity of the old reading; then by proposing something, which to superficial readers would seem specious, but which the editor rejects with indignation; then by producing the true reading, with a long paraphrase, and concluding with loud acclamations on the discovery, and a sober wish for the advancement and prosperity of genuine criticism.

DR. JOHNSON: *Preface to Shakespeare*

TRUE scholarship is a noble, selfless and touching pursuit. It can exist only on a high level of civilization; and perhaps the valuing of knowledge for its own sake is one of the tests of a civilization. The willingness of professional scholars to help one another, and not only one another, but people like myself who have no pretension to real scholarship, has to be seen to be believed; there seems to be a world fraternity of such people and a desire for knowledge is a passport to the most disinterested kindness, the most careful guidance; it has often made me feel very reverent and humble. It is possible for someone to devote a lifetime to Icelandic literature or Ben Jonson or prosody; and it is well that this should be so, for the supreme scholars set the standard for all other teachers and students.

However, there is a place for everything; and the place for the austerity of scholarship is not in books for the ordinary school child. Comparatively few people are interested in the minute details of literary study, and the average school child is bored by an annotated edition of a Shakespeare play. He, and still more she, will memorize annotations with exemplary patience and even reproduce them in examinations; by threats, bribes, appeals to vanity or the teaching drive that depends on personality, most children can be taught almost anything in the sense of being able to repeat it; but the number of real scholars in the population does not appear to be much on the increase. As a child I was fairly interested in annotations; but I happened to be the kind of child who is fond of reading by nature. And in the miserable husks of mis-education which made up most of my education till I was sixteen, a reading child will read anything in the hope of extracting some flavour from it. Probably most people are still miserably mis-educated.

One of the advantages of studying a modern play, such as Drinkwater's *Abraham Lincoln* or Shaw's *Saint Joan*, both of which have been used for examination purposes, though Shaw is said to have refused to allow any of his plays to be edited as set books on humanitarian grounds, is that the annotator has not much to do. There is no obsolete diction to be paraphrased, no historical allusion to which the reader cannot obtain access in books generally available, no code of honour or morality so different from that at present in force as to be incomprehensible. The reader has to apply his or her own intelligence to anything that is not understood and bring his or her own judgment to the problems of character and conduct. What is modern is not necessarily, as has been too often supposed, a 'soft option'; it may demand more of a reader's intelligence, maturity and critical faculty, if less of his memorizing powers, than an old play; and memory is, after all, a mechanical faculty not invariably found in conjunction with high intelligence. It is more satisfying and certainly more truly educative to think things out for ourselves than to open bird-like beaks for successive spoonfuls of predigested information. Indeed, most of us will see examples, if we have not already done so, of the use of annotations paralysing someone's critical faculty. I have often suspected that one of the reasons for the popularity

174

of Shakespeare in schools—with teachers—is that he nowadays needs notes. Many people whose task is supposed to be to teach the appreciation of literature can find nothing to say about a modern play and nothing to do with it; and the common convention that there is one set play for a public examination, or the more horrifying convention that one play must last a class for a term[1] makes it necessary to study something from which a great deal of talk and a great many exercises can be extracted. Consequently it is possible for Shakespeare, who is as much worth studying as any author in the world and who offers an unrivalled array of interesting stories, good jokes, lifelike characters, verbal beauty and human wisdom, to become dull and lifeless, a piece of chewing-gum from which all the sugar and flavouring have long been extracted. At any intellectual level it is possible to study one book too long, especially if the study is continuous.

Probably the best way for a student to counteract the mentally clogging effects of a too mechanical use of notes is to treat the script being studied as a potential production—it is better still if we can actually produce it—and treat the notes as aids to the producer. All examination candidates feel short of time and, if intelligent, feel that there are many things they would like to do if only they had time; notes save a great deal of lengthy though interesting research and are indispensable if several set plays are to be done in a year. The candidate who feels that my approach takes a great deal of time may be comforted by the thought that we remember more clearly and for a longer time what we have worked out for ourselves than what we have merely memorized parrot-fashion.

If notes are treated as aids to production, many that look dull become quite exciting and give rise to spirited argument. This kind of note is very helpful to the producer:

[1] This wearisome need is caused partly by the need to be moderate in expenditure on textbooks, and is thus not wholly avoidable.

Whatso'er you will employ me in,
Were it to call King Edward's widow sister,
I will perform it.

Richard III, Act I, Sc. 1

Dr. Johnson's note: "This is a very covert and subtle manner of insinuating treason. The natural expression would have been, *were it to call King Edward's* wife *sister*. I will solicit for you though it should be at the expense of so much degradation and constraint, as to own the low-born wife of King Edward for a sister. But by slipping as it were casually *widow* into the place of *wife*, he tempts Clarence with an oblique proposal to kill the king."

We could miss this. Clearly in reciting the speech there should be some slight, significant hesitation before the word 'widow', or perhaps, some slight stress on it. This note may be essential to a student who does not yet know *Richard II* well:

Richard: Most mighty prince, my Lord Northumberland,
What says King Bolingbroke?

Richard II, Act III, Sc. 3

Note in a school edition of 1890: Said with ironical humility. There are real difficulties in the interpretation of the character of Richard II, especially by an inexperienced person, for it is not only a part to be acted, but the part of a man who himself likes to be theatrical. This double theatricalism, which could easily be mistaken by the student for the heightened speech to be found in any drama, is difficult to grasp and such a note is useful.

The student is advised to shun, however, the unhealthy and gloomy habit of reading a set play with one finger in the section of notes at the end and turning every now and then to this small-print section to see if anything in the scene just read has an annotation to be learned. The whole concept of 'set books' could, with some advantages to the teaching of literature, be critically queried and the method perhaps revised extensively; but certainly finger-in-end is the very worst way of studying such a book. The student

176

should remember that a play which was ever performed could once be absorbed, at least fully enough to give great enjoyment, by an average audience, in the time it took to perform it, and that people actually paid to see it. Even when some allowance has been made for the passage of time obscuring what once was clear, it is best to read the play first several times without looking at the notes at all. The ideal way to use notes would be as follows: to embark, after several enjoyable and progressively careful readings of the play, on a slow reading of it with the intention that this time nothing should remain obscure; to halt at the first line not confidently understood, and—to attack it for oneself. If the problem was simply a word not known, the dictionary or a Shakespeare glossary might suffice; a large dictionary with some account of the changes in the meaning of words should be used; the *Shorter Oxford English Dictionary* is a good one for the purpose, and the immense row of volumes of which this is a summary would be better still if possible. Other problems might be solved by a thoughtful student by examining the line(s) from the point of view of grammar, known character of the speaker, historical background and dramatic situation; such reference books as books on history and on English historical costume might help much. Several students, combining to discuss a series of problems, might learn much more than one student working alone.

Often the problem would be solved and the solution vivid in the memory for months, as are most things we work out for ourselves; the student who thought the problem was solved could then turn to the notes and see what a more experienced editor had to say. Often the two answers would coincide; sometimes the student would be proved wrong and learn something new by seeing the mistake. If a problem seemed insoluble after an honest effort, then the student could turn in despair to the notes at the back much as we 'cheat' when we cannot solve a puzzle in a book and turn to the answers. This would have another advantage; anyone who had wrestled with the difficulty and learned its complexity by experiment would truly appreciate the ingenuity of the person who would solve the problems, and respect for scholarship would be enhanced.

Conversely, intelligent students would be spared the annoyance of those irritating statements of the obvious which sometimes masquerade as notes in school editions and serve I presume, to make the book fatter and more costly:

> And when I mount, alive may I not light,
> If I be traitor or unjustly fight!
>
> *Richard II*, Act I, Sc. 1

Note to school edition, 1890: mount: sc. my horse, such combats being on horseback.

Now, if anyone is about to fight in a public trial by combat in England, and is going to mount anything, is there really any risk that a person intelligent enough to read Shakespeare at all may be tempted to suppose that he might intend to mount a clothes-horse, a camel, a bicycle or a steam-roller? If notes are not used mechanically each student can take what is needed from the back, for levels of intelligence differ. One of the advantages of treating set plays as real plays intended to be produced is that it removes some of the necessity for notes, in that much which is puzzling in print immediately explains itself in action or when we try to read it aloud.

Children and students, I believe, ought to learn to read fast and gluttonously, instead of slowly with many artificial hindrances to appetite; but examinations have their uses and their special demands. The fierce arguments and passionate ardours of production, the more moderate warmth of lively discussion, are antidotes to an over-academic, arid approach to a set play. Let no one, tired of studying annotations or poring over one text for too long, jump to the conclusion that Shakespeare or any other great dramatist is a ponderous old bore. There is much dullness generated about them; some people have a dreadful gift for making anything they touch dull; but the dramatists are vividly, violently alive, much more alive than many of us dare to be.

178

Part Three

DRAMA AS LIVING EXPERIENCE

XIII. INTERPRETATION AS AN AID TO STUDY

> . . . this player here,
> But in a fiction, in a dream of passion,
> Could force his soul so to his own conceit,
> That, from her working, all his visage wann'd;
> Tears in his eyes, distraction in's aspect,
> A broken voice, and his whole function suiting
> With forms to his conceit. . . .
>
> *Hamlet*, Act II, Sc. 2

THE way to study the script of a play sensibly, as it is one of the chief purposes of this book to insist, is to see it as a potential production and, if possible, to see it produced or, better still, to produce it. One caution is needed for the inexperienced student, especially with regard to a professional production that may be visited. The more complex and subtle a play is, the more likely it is that views on the proper interpretation of it will differ. If plays did not present problems of interpretation, people would not write notes on them. Two people drawing a landscape may emphasize different features; two people playing a piece of music may differ considerably from each other, not only in skill but in two interpretations both of which can be justified by the score; two people, even, who bake a cake using the same recipe, and both being competent, will not turn out exactly identical cakes. The interpretation of a play is bound to be even more liable to variations, since it depends not on one person but on a team.

The variations in interpretation are likely to be greater in old plays than in contemporary plays, because the old plays have very few stage directions. The use of stage directions has steadily increased until now some publishers of plays cultivate a habit of minute and almost continuous directions until the printed script looks something like this:

Mary: (*moving away from the bookcase and sitting down on* R. *of sofa*) Well, can we sit down and (*with diffidence*) talk it over?

Jane: (*who has been tapping her foot uneasily during the last speech*) Talk? (*Wipes nose.*) I don't know that talking will do much good. (*Pause*) But I am quite willing. (*Leaves fireplace and sits in armchair.*)

Mary: (*putting one foot on top of the other*) I do want to be reasonable. (*Sighs*)

Jane: (*lighting a cigarette*) Most of us do. The fact remains that we both claim the same house, and all the documents are missing. (*Draws hard on cigarette and puffs smoke out with a nervous gesture.*)

Mary: (*uncrossing her legs and leaning forward*) You know that I really have nowhere else to go?

Jane: (*abruptly*) I have some sense of decency. (*Shakes ash off her cigarette.*) There is no question of throwing you out into the rain.[1]

Such over-directed scripts leave the producer no discretion, frequently worry and distract the cast more than they help, and are very difficult to read silently, though this last is not an important defect. Such acting editions are a danger to the art of the producer by making it look easy, when in fact play production even at an amateur standard is a delicate and difficult art. The good actor or actress—aided by a good producer—should be able to find suitable movement and gesture for a part; the nature of the character to be portrayed should dictate the right kind of movement. In Shakespeare we find directions only where the producer needs guidance on vitally significant actions that must on no account be omitted: 'Stabs him'; 'Smothers her'; 'Sleeps'; 'Scattering flowers'; 'Sleeps; Iachimo comes from the

---

[1] This is an imaginary fragment.

trunk'; 'Swoons' and the old favourite from *The Winter's Tale*, 'Exit, pursued by a bear'.[1] Moreover, there were even fewer directions in the old plays as they were first written; some of them we owe to later editors. The same economy of stage directions is practised by such moderns as T. S. Eliot and Christopher Fry. Shaw gives very full descriptions of rooms, persons and vital actions, but leaves the producer plenty of scope for inventions and credits him with some intelligence. On the other hand, when an old dramatist is describing a masque, show, vision, procession or other spectacle, or when a modern dramatist wants a complicated action, special lighting effect or unusual setting, as many details of stage direction as are needed to ensure accuracy must be used, and it is then the producer's task to carry out these requirements as closely as possible.

If we go to a performance of a play in order to know more about it—which is a very good way of studying a play —we must also beware of concluding that what we see is exactly what the author intended. We must also not assume, unless the production is obviously a hopelessly bad one, that the interpretation is far removed from what the author intended or that of two not hopeless productions one is far better than the other. If a production is consistent within itself, has been adequately rehearsed by a well-chosen cast (serious under-rehearsal becomes obvious to even an inexperienced spectator), seems coherent and has convincing physical adjuncts—costume, lighting, scenery and properties—it has at least some merits both as entertainment and as education.

Most of the argument about interpretation that is heard outside the professional theatre concerns Shakespeare, partly because Shakespeare's plays include some of the most subtle and problematical characters imaginable and partly because, since most good producers at some time try their hand on Shakespeare, the ordinary playgoer is more likely

[1] It has been suggested that this idea originated in the current handiness of a bear-pit.

Drama as Living Experience

to have seen several versions of a Shakespeare play than of anything else. There are special problems attached to producing Shakespeare today: many of the words he used are no longer used or have changed in meaning; in some places there is controversy as to what the correct script is; and sometimes it is not clear what the script means. Shakespeare's plays were written for a theatre constructed differently from those of today and for a different style of acting. Such problems are less serious in plays of the eighteenth century or later.

To watch any production intelligently is to learn a great deal, not about the one and perfect way in which a play should be produced, for there is no such thing, but about the problems that have to be solved. To watch a production with such things consciously in mind is not how we normally go to the theatre; the ideal way to have our first experience of a play is to see it in the theatre without having read the script, which is what the author intended, and thus to receive its full psychological impact and be steeped in the illusion; but if we have the opportunity of seeing a play which we have studied, we probably know the words more or less by heart, or at least well enough to recognize them as familiar when spoken, and we are not in suspense about the actual story. Then the following points may be useful topics for discussion afterwards.

1. *Unexpected Interpretation of Character*

If we have studied a Shakespeare play at all closely we have some idea in our head of how we should interpret each character; but our idea is usually inadequate or even quite wrong. When we see a production we may observe that an actor treats the character quite differently from our concept. We may react immediately by saying, 'Well, what a fool I was!'

For instance, we may have pictured Richard III as merely a crook-backed monster; a great actor in the part can make us realize also his dreadful fascination—as in the wonderful

184

wooing scene with Lady Anne—and his intellectual liveliness. We may be so hypnotized by the grace of his language, especially if an inept teacher once told us to admire it, that we do not feel the weakness, sentimentality and vacillation of Richard II. Sir Andrew Aguecheek is one of the most gloriously silly characters in Shakespeare, inspired in all he does and says with a divine ineptitude; it is all there in the script, but I never saw it until I attended a performance of the play. There are several possible interpretations of such characters as Hamlet, Cleopatra, Isabella, Desdemona or Macbeth, not only in details of production but in the whole pattern of the character. This is not carelessness in Shakespeare; for is it not true that every character we meet in real life remains very largely a mystery? Not only does the tone of voice and its inflections stress the facets of the personality being portrayed in a given production; movement, costume and make-up all contribute something.

It would be an excellent exercise for a group of students confronted with a set play to divide into smaller groups with each group rehearsing the same two or three important scenes quite independently of the others, and then act or play-read them in succession; a discussion afterwards, among fairly intelligent people, would produce a flood of comment on the play itself.

2. *Setting*

It is always interesting to see what a producer does in the way of scenery, lighting and properties, musical effects and any other devices that can be used to make a play more beautiful and convincing. Many of the devices used in a professional production are out of reach of schoolchildren or students, and this is one of the minor reasons why it is useful to see a professional production when studying a set play. Beautiful painted scenery, a startlingly lovely room, weird, ethereal or realistic lighting, sumptuous costumes or interestingly experimental ones, can all contribute to the interest of a play and are worthy of study. For instance, the

185

skill and tact with which the thunderstorm is suggested is very important in *King Lear*; a good one is merely what is expected, but a bad one may spoil the whole play by causing embarrassment. In many plays of Shakespeare musical effects are required even according to the early stage directions, such as 'Hautboys under the stage'.[1] But the student who is interested in this technical side of production must remember that many of the resources of a modern producer would have seemed to Shakespeare like magic; he was writing for a stage with very little equipment of any kind. There have been very beautiful productions of Shakespeare which are quite unlike anything Shakespeare could possibly have visualized, though that does not mean he would not probably have been delighted with them. It is legitimate to be thrilled by lovely effects using modern techniques, but also wise to remember that a great play does not depend on such things for its emotional excitement and mental stimulus.

3. *Cutting*

When we see a Shakespeare or other sixteenth-, seventeenth- or possibly even eighteenth-century play produced for the first time, we shall, if we know the script well, notice a number of omissions and alterations. This is because such a play is too long as it stands for production in the theatre of the present day, partly because of the intervals and scene-shifting of the modern theatre. We can learn a good deal from noticing these cuts and trying to understand why the producer, faced with the necessity of cutting somewhere, chose these lines.

4. *Textual Criticism*

Textual Criticism is the science-cum-art of examining an old printed book or manuscript in an attempt to find the right version of something that does not seem right as it stands, or of which there are several suggested versions. This is needed mostly for old books, as the standard of printing

[1] 'Hautboys' are now spelt 'oboes'.

nowadays is high and mistakes are usually corrected before a book is published. The textual critic removes any obvious printer's errors or meaningless interpolations; he compares all the available texts of a book to find the likeliest readings in places where there are different versions (*collation*); when, after consultation of dictionaries and works of reference, he can find no possible meaning for the words as they stand, he alters them to give some sensible meaning that he can justify (*emendation*); and he provides footnotes to explain anything in the text that has a meaning as it stands but would not otherwise be clear to the uninformed reader (*annotation*). (This is what is meant by the *editing* of an old book.) This work, especially when described in this over-simple manner, for which I hope textual scholars may forgive me, may sound very dull, but it is more interesting than it sounds and is essential for the right understanding of old plays—and other old books.

The person who nowadays prints an edition of a play script for the use of examination candidates has the duty of presenting the textual problems fairly and, having chosen one possible reading, must indicate the other possible versions in the notes and give a short account of the evidence for the correctness of each. The producer, on the other hand, certainly cannot allow the actor to say each of several possible readings in succession; he has to make up his mind and allow one chosen reading to be used with any actions that are implied. From a production we can, therefore, often test the dramatic fitness of a particular reading and see how it fits in with the other speeches. A crux from *King Lear* may provide a suitable example:

(*Kent is reading a letter and is seated in the stocks.*)
Kent: I know 'tis from Cordelia,
    Who hath most fortunately been inform'd
    Of my obscured course; and shall find time
    From this enormous state, seeking to give
    Losses their remedies
                                                    Act I, Sc. 2

187

Drama as Living Experience

A few moments later Kent falls asleep. Now, though the gist of this is clearly that Cordelia has heard from Kent and intends to put right all that has gone wrong in England, the speech as it stands is not grammatical and does not make unmistakably clear sense. What actual words did Shakespeare intend? It has been suggested, and accepted by Dr. Johnson as a possibility, that the lines should read 'enormous state-seeking', the state-seeking referring to Cordelia's need to provide for herself after being disowned, and thus meaning that once Cordelia is well established as Queen of France she will see if she can spare time to help her father. But as Johnson says, 'This is harsh!' it does not fit our idea of Cordelia as a loving daughter with a strong sense of duty. Some editors suggest that the obscure lines are a fragment of Cordelia's letter read aloud by Kent:

> Who hath most fortunately been inform'd
> Of my obscured course; and 'shall find time
> From this enormous state, seeking to give
> Losses their remedies.'

Thus the lines would mean '(I)—shall find time from the great cares of state in France, seeking to remedy all losses', or just possibly, '(I)—shall find time to do something about this enormous (i.e. related to 'enormity') state of affairs in England'. Some alter the apparently ungrammatical 'shall' to 'she'll', which may well be right and improves the sense, but still does not make it clear how we are to take 'state-seeking. . . .' A last suggestion, and one which is very tempting to the practical producer, is that Kent, who has just said he is tired and is about to fall asleep, is already showing signs of sleepiness and that the troublesome lines represent the vague mumblings of a tired man.

It is also not unusual to omit in production, whenever possible, lines containing awkward or obsolete expressions; some producers substitute a more familiar word, which is probably a good policy if it is done by someone with a good ear for language.

Interpretation as an Aid to Study

5. Explanation of Words in Production

It is not unusual to learn for the first time what a word or phrase means or what the point of it is when we see the play produced. This is especially true of old plays in which changes of language are an obstacle to understanding. It is often true of Shakespearian puns, for quite a small change in pronunciation can destroy a pun completely. The actor may modify pronunciation in order to bring out a pun, or revive old pronunciation such as the *i-on* ending in order to keep the right rhythm.

Another and really much more important way in which a production can throw light on the meaning of words is by movement, gesture and intonation, showing the dramatic significance of expressions when we had missed it.

> There's matter in these sighs, these profound heaves:
> You must translate; 'tis fit we understand them.
>
> *Hamlet*, Act IV, Sc. 1

These lines sound rather insignificant at a first reading, a mere introduction to a scene; but if we treat the script as full of hints for the production of a play, there is a direction here for effective 'business'. On the stage, the Queen can be left alone as Hamlet drags the body of Polonius away, after bitterly rebuking her. She is now overcome with remorse, fear and bewilderment and shows her distress by crying, sighing and sobbing. We are given the impression of someone whose self-control has broken; the King comes in and, seeing her condition, knows that there may be danger to himself in anything she lets out. He stands watching; instead of running to comfort her, he insists on knowing the details. His brutal practical attitude is contrasted with her helpless distress and feeble defence of her son. (This interpretation ignores an act division; but on the modern stage the two scenes are telescoped, and in Shakespeare's day there were no curtains and probably no break.)

189

Drama as Living Experience

Similarly this rather banal verse has good dramatic possibilities for an imaginative actress:

Hermia: (*awaking*) Help me, Lysander! help me! do thy best
        To pluck this crawling serpent from my breast.
        Ay me, for pity! what a dream was here!
        Lysander, look how I do quake with fear:
        Methought a serpent ate my heart away,
        And you sat smiling at his cruel prey.—
        Lysander!—what, removed? Lysander! lord!—
        What, out of hearing? gone? no sound, no word?
        Alack, where are you? speak, an if you hear;
        Speak, of all loves! I swoon almost with fear.
        No? then I well perceive you are not nigh:
        Either death or you I'll find immediately.
        (*Exit*)

In most of the disguises and consequent talk at cross-purposes so frequent in Shakespeare, there are possible bits of 'business' which emphasize the comicality, or, occasionally, the pathos of the situation, and may show the point of a speech much more clearly than a silent reading.

There is much less action in Milton's two plays, which are about as undramatic as a produceable play can be and the second of which was never intended for public performance; but both can be performed and even here a line is sometimes clearer in production than in reading:

    That hallo I should know, what are you? speak;
    Com not too neer, you fall on iron stakes else.

                       Comus

may be misread as a warning that the Spirit who is approaching is in danger of tripping over a spiked fence; in production we see the two brothers draw their swords and take up a posture of defence; the 'iron stakes' has a twist of grim half-humour not uncommon in Milton. The scream of slaughtered Philistines is much more obvious and horrifying in a production of *Samson Agonistes* than in the script.

Interpretation as an Aid to Study

6. *The Intensification of Emotion*

Production is the true test of a play; and, especially when studying a script with the minuteness of detail required for examinations, we may repeatedly read it so slowly that its emotional impact is lost. Producing or reading it ourselves may not altogether remedy this, for if the play has not already made a strong impression, either tragic or comic, we cannot really wish to act it or to convey the emotion. Another very real difficulty for the young student of great drama is that many of the emotions—the mixed motives and wild sublimity of the death of Cleopatra, the feverish guilty hallucinations of the dagger scene in *Macbeth*, the passion-charged self-control of Viola talking to the Duke in *Twelfth Night*, the ardour and sincerity of Imogen in the changing crises of an eventful story, or, to go outside Shakespeare, the terrible calm of the Duchess of Malfi after enduring so much that she is without hope, the intellectual arrogance of Faustus, the impatient insight of Saint Joan, may be so far outside the range of emotions yet experienced as to be incomprehensible. Here the sight of a fine production may give a great deal of help and may completely transform our experience of the play. This, however, is an exception to the other aids mentioned above; from such an experience we do not gain intellectual illumination or a stimulating urge to discuss points of criticism; we acquire a deeper and more important knowledge simply by being overwhelmed.

191

XIV. DRAMA IS NATURAL

Then will he fit his tongue
To dialogues of business, love or strife;
But it will not be long
Ere this be thrown aside,
And with new joy and pride
The little Actor cons another part;
Filling from time to time his 'humorous stage'
With all the Persons, down to palsied Age,
That Life brings with her in her equipage;
As if his whole vocation
Were endless imitation.

WORDSWORTH: *Ode on Intimations of Immortality*

MOST people think they never act. If they were asked, 'Have you any experience of acting?' they would reply, 'No', and sometimes add some scornful or wistful comment. Drama is usually thought of as a cultural activity; it is something that we did at school, or do in a society, or something that other people do to entertain us for a treat. Yet in fact drama is almost as natural to human beings as breathing—and, for reasons of physical illness or nervous troubles, many of us also do not breathe properly!

'Let's pretend . . .' says the child; and imaginative play is almost universal among children. Educationists and psychologists such as Susan Isaacs and Margaret Lowenfeld have demonstrated that we can often learn much about a child's personality by observing its play; we can see what is troubling the child, or what wishes it tries to satisfy in 'pretend' games; it is now believed that this kind of dramatic play is an important factor in intellectual growth. The very young child occupies himself in imaginative play by himself; he chuffs round the room being a train or crawls on the floor

Drama is Natural

being a puppy or a kitten. Older children get into groups to play 'pretend' games and often, either in school or in the home, show a remarkable degree of teamwork and co-operation in playing 'houses' or 'schools' or 'cowboys and Indians'. Indeed, it is often curiously touching to see the concentration, the selfless absorption, with which children act out these little dramas, ill-constructed and often ill-informed, but wonderfully sincere and direct. An intelligent child in the dreadful powerlessness of childhood may often remain sane very largely because it can act. The child who has been smacked is much consoled by re-enacting the story with herself in the mother's role and the doll in her own. 'Pretend' play can be very elaborate and some imaginative children show great persistence and intelligence in it; perhaps most children would continue it for longer if they were not encouraged by adults into formal team games.

We usually think that 'pretend' games are confined to children, but this is not so. Thurber's brilliant short story, *The Secret Life of Walter Mitty*—now well known in a film version which is, however, less perfect—is a clever study of an unhappy adult's fantasy life. In 'pretend' games we can at all ages aspire to satisfactions that are out of reach in real life.

Dramatic work is used a good deal nowadays in the cure of mental and nervous disorders, a fact which seems to support the view that 'pretend' games are a valuable outlet for our feelings. Some psychiatrists encourage their patients to 'act out' things that have distressed them and this is now sometimes done in groups so that the members of the group have also the advantage of helping each other and working in co-operation. But all of us are acting in quite another way for a large part of our lives. At work or with some of our acquaintance wherever there is a considerable mixture of generations or of cultures, in an uncongenial community or in some post of responsibility we have to act in order to spare people pain, keep the peace or protect ourselves. Students of Jung may like to relate this to the concept of the

Drama as Living Experience

Persona. We almost all have to wear a mask over our real personality in our social life; sometimes we need several interchangeable masks. This social need can easily turn into a false, hypocritical, self-deceiving way of life; it is perhaps least harmful when we recognize it for what it is—acting, for the sake of stability in life. Then we may even begin to take an artistic interest in it and resent its needs less fiercely.

Drama is also deeply rooted in magic, religion and ritual. So far as we know it originated always in man's attempts to explain the obvious mysteries of life, to propitiate the forces that seemed to control them and to enforce a system of ethics by an appeal to supernatural authority. In some very primitive communities a man will perform a dance in which he mimes the capture of the animal he wishes to capture, or will pour liquid on the ground as an example to the rain-god when rain is wanted. (The first at least is psychologically sound; how many of us have been told to go into an interview for a coveted post as if we had already got it?) Anyone who cares to read books on anthropology will find many other examples of the dramatization of something we want to happen as a religious rite among primitive peoples. Traces of this survive in European superstitions, such as turning over our money at the new moon in order to have plenty of money to turn!

The formal drama originated in religious festivals. The Greek drama, which eventually included some of the greatest tragedies the world has yet known, developed out of the rituals of the annual festival of Dionysius, though the exact details of how this happened are still uncertain. British drama began with bits of dialogue (The Trope) intended to make the Easter celebrations in church more vivid and impressive; and it is known that there were religious and ritual origins for the Jewish drama, the Chinese drama, all European Christian drama and probably the Indian drama; in South America the conquering Spaniards brought Miracle Plays to Indians who already had a dramatic tradition that had developed out of their primitive cults. What happened

194

in Europe and, with modifications, elsewhere, was that a ritual was made more impressive and lucid by introducing a fragment of dialogue and perhaps dignified mime; this was such a success that it developed gradually into something longer, into a little play; gradually the play developed into an elaborate art form and became secularized, until in many countries a paradoxical opposition between Church and Stage developed, examples of this being seen in Puritan England and in Catholic France in the time of Molière. The earliest acting was done by priests and their assistants, and one of the causes of the increasing secularization of the drama was that laymen had soon to be called in to fill parts in the expanding 'cast'. As the drama became a form of secular entertainment its scope widened—naturally love scenes and battles cannot properly be represented in a church—and also it became more self-consciously artistic, until in the late seventeenth century nearly every play had a prologue asking for the goodwill of the critics. Today acting is recognized as a liberal profession and a lofty vocation.

Ritual as known today still includes an element of drama; a marriage service with its symbolic actions and vows, a funeral service, a commemoration service, a degree ceremony, a military parade or a coronation have obvious bits of drama in them. An instinctive love of acting, both of taking part in drama and of watching it, seems to be one of our genuine social and psychological needs. (Most people in any kind of authority know the value of a little ceremony in bringing a community together when it is disintegrating.) The healthful effect of dramatic work on children and students is usually very noticeable. Acting or play-reading increases their poise and self-confidence; it seems to stimulate intelligence and aids the development of such social virtues as co-operation, helpfulness and responsibility; it improves the voice and therefore often makes it easier for the student to be articulate and fluent in conversation; there is some evidence that it also helps emotional development on deeper levels. For our present civilization is rather afraid of strong emotions and

Drama as Living Experience

when we are taught too soon to hide them we may become incapable of feeling them again until they are restored to us by the experience of acting strong emotional parts.

Moreover, drama is the only art which is still inescapably communal. Poetry can be written for a small cultured minority and even, perhaps, gain in some respects thereby; prose of any kind is normally read in silence and privacy; but a play needs a group of actors to interpret it and usually has an audience to respond to it. A communal experience can be very satisfying, though people who are unable to be alone are as sick in mind as those who fear to be in society. If the desire for collective experience is not satisfied in such harmless and often beneficial ways as organized worship, innocuous public ceremonies, drama, community singing (and other musical activities), excursions, harmless societies and team games, there is a risk that it may take such forms as howling for the blood of Jews, lynching, or marching to war. To play any part in the creation of a play, as author, actor, producer or stagehand, is to take part in a communal experience of a worth-while, creative kind.

Drama, at its best, is an exercise of the imagination not only for writer, producer and actors but also for the audience. The writer of plays creates characters and places them in situations that are interesting and in some way relevant to general human experience. He says to us, as it were, 'Look, this is a sample of life for you; isn't it sad? Isn't it grand?' or 'Isn't it a scream?' Or, less commonly, he may ask, 'What would you have done?' Or even, 'What are you going to do about this?' The actor tries to live for a short time as another person and enter into the feelings and thoughts of an imaginary character, thus not only increasing his range of imagined experience but probably deepening his own personal life.

But the audience forms the third side of the great triangle of responses which is drama, and this is the side on which the student is most often found. The intelligent and co-operative audience is submitting itself to a new experience, accepting a sample of life and tasting it, sharing in the lives of imaginary people not altogether unlike known live persons. Out of that experience there should come deeper insight, wider sympathies and an increase of charity; but there is also a sense of relief. Aristotle spoke of the tragic *catharsis*, the purging by pity and fear; there is a kind of harmless discharge of emotion; we are moved by imagined painful events, but this does not distress us as it would if they were known to be real. Similarly, it is natural though unethical to laugh at people who are ridiculous; to do this much in real life would brand as callous and despicable; but on the stage ridiculous people may be seen in embarrassing situations and we laugh with no sense of guilt. Indeed, we know that the more we laugh the more the actors will be pleased. We may also sometimes feel relief at being able to laugh at things which in real life are not at all funny, such as the broken marriages of Restoration comedy or the crime in Priestley's *Laburnum Grove*.

Drama is thus an expression of instinctive desires, a valuable outlet and a rich educational experience; and it has the loftiest associations; but it is also necessary for the student of drama to recognize that today there is a commercial drama just as there is commercial fiction, that is, a drama that is written and staged primarily in the hope of earning money, and whose audience assembles chiefly in the hope of an evening's diversion. It is very prevalent in England today, but this is not at all the only age, or the worst, in which it has been seen. There is nothing dishonourable in commercial drama unless it is artistically or morally so debased as seriously to degrade taste, like the shallow melodramas of the nineteenth century or the revolting spectacles of the decadence in Ancient Rome. The drama that provides mere amusement, 'escape', wish-fulfilment, distraction, is as useful and as harmful as the detective story, the crossword, the inferior film, the bridge game; it provides a relief for strained and tired minds and bodies; all pleasure is good so long as it does no positive harm; but these diversions can, with some people, become a stupid and meaningless addiction.

True, there is the additional disadvantage that 'bad money drives out good'; what might be desirable is a system of theatre organization in which both diversion and genuine art were always available in every town, just as the Light Programme and the Third Programme of the B.B.C. cater for the two needs; but when most of the managers of the big theatres find it most profitable to produce plays or shows that do nothing to stir our deeper emotions or stimulate our intellects, the good plays may lie in script neglected; and that is a real loss. However, it is possible to be priggish about commercial drama; if people really feel the need for mere distraction they should have it, and at present there is plenty of more important and interesting dramatic activity in Britain. Tripe is an innocuous diet for the sick, though the healthy soon tire of it; unhappily the precariousness of civilization at present, fear of war, repressive education, lack of privacy, an exaggerated value set on wealth and success, constant hustle, and a continuing suspicion of love and tenderness, do produce a good many sick minds.

As students of the drama we are concerned mostly with that drama which has permanent literary value, sometimes called the legitimate drama, and it will generally be found that if it has real literary merit it also has emotional force, intellectual interest, a high standard of wit, if appropriate, and some set of stated or implied values. It is necessary to remember that artistic and commercial drama are not found on opposite sides of a rigid Golden Curtain; as in all questions of taste or morality there is far more grey in the world than black or white. Most dramatists have written in part for money; it seems certain that Shakespeare himself did; and indeed, to be divorced from any need to make money out of their work seems to be harmful to authors as often as it is helpful; someone who does not have to earn a living is immediately cut off from one of the continuously important aspects of normal life, and his view of life may become un-

real or distorted. Money is not the only criterion; it is not
difficult to tell a play which gives nothing but diversion from
a play that has more to offer, and plenty of plays, including
those of the greatest dramatists, include both elements.

One of the essentially pathetic facts about human life is
that, as far as we know, we have only one rather short life
and the possibilities of experience in one life are very small.
We can normally have only one kind of career, one type of
body, one temperament, one marriage (if that), a few children (if any), one nationality, one religion (if any), one political affiliation, one kind of home and one kind of death;
and every decision we make in a given situation is irrever-
sible; we can never go back and take the left fork in the road
instead of the right, or see what would have happened if
we had plucked that golden bough instead of pursuing that
blue bird. The variations possible for one person are limited
even when variations are possible at all. We have none of us
much idea what it is like to be someone else. All through life
we have to make choices which limit us further; we have to
let many things and, worse, people go we should like to
study, seek, change, love or serve, simply because we have
not the time or the ability. In acting or going to see plays
we can live many lives by proxy and so have at least the
illusion of widening our experience; this is very satisfying.
We can have, by proxy and in perfect safety, exciting, critical
experiences; we can feel tremendous storms of emotion such
as it is hardly held permissible to experience in real life; we
can be both respectable and criminal, mad and sane, loving
and isolated, old and young; we can even change our sex;
we can also, in comedy, make fools of ourselves, and this too
is satisfying, for there is a hidden clown in the staidest of us
and, too, we may unconsciously believe that by acting the
fool we propitiate the ancient gods and they will spare us the
ignominy of looking fools at some time when it is not convenient! Lastly, the writer of drama, even of a drama created
in the classroom or the home for strictly local consumption
becomes more than human for a time, and, as we all wish

199

Drama as Living Experience

in our more reckless moments, becomes an omnipotent, omniscient and gloriously irresponsible creator who makes persons and destroys them, moves them about with ruthless indifference and nevertheless is doing no harm to fill him later with self-questioning and remorse. The satisfactions of every kind of creation are deep and lasting; but possibly the drama offers the most intense satisfactions of all.

In view of the immense satisfaction to be had from anything to do with plays—the releases of repressed emotions, the excitements of creation, the violent emotional impacts that give sharp and unforgettable pleasure, the enrichment brought by collective experience, the increasing of imagination, feeling and sympathy and the development of enquiry and speculation, as well as the pure aesthetic pleasure of the theatre—it is not surprising that the life-haters, the puritans, the narrow-minded, the people who fear and hate happiness and human sympathy, are violent and continuous opponents of the theatre even more than of the other arts. This may in part account for the practice of studying plays as scripts only in many schools and colleges, for many details in the history of education may be explained by the perpetual war, nowadays as marked in education as in any field, between the puritans, the life-haters, and the humanists and creators, a war in which some compromise has often been necessary. All the arts are a menace to the puritan; they give pleasure and they stimulate an interest in full and sincere living; but the theatre is the most dangerous because its impact is the most violent and immediate. The arts are alive; and for the puritan it is so much easier and safer to be dead.

SUGGESTIONS FOR FURTHER READING

The Oxford Companion to the Theatre and *The Oxford Companion to English Literature* are two great reference books that between them probably contain all the information about the drama from a historical point of view that the non-specialist student can possibly want. They are both arranged alphabetically, are miraculously cheap for the amount of information packed into them, and are very well produced. They should be in every school or college library, but are also well worth owning for the private person who has any interest in literature. The *Companion to the Theatre* is at present the more up-to-date and contains much information about world theatre and theatrical technique as well as more literary data.

Allardyce Nicoll's four invaluable books, *World Drama*, *British Drama*, *Readings from British Drama* and *The Development of the Theatre*, in themselves make a miniature reference library.

The reader who wants lists of books on specific aspects of the drama will find a long bibliography at the end of *The Oxford Companion to the Theatre*, and the National Book League issues two excellent lists, *British Drama: History and Criticism* (1/–) and *Shakespeare* (1/6).

The British Drama League, 9 Fitzroy Square, London, W.1, has a reference and lending library of 90,000 volumes, publishes a valuable quarterly magazine, *Drama* (2/–) and advises on various subjects to do with the drama. It is possible for organizations as well as individuals to join it.

Suggestions for Further Reading

THE PLAYS THEMSELVES

While the best way to enjoy a play is undoubtedly to see it and the best way to make a close study of it is to perform it, this is not always practical; wide reading will supplement actual theatre experience. This very modest list gives some of the essentials for a general view of the British drama.

1. *Early Plays*

Some Miracle and Morality Plays, notably *Everyman*, plus, if possible, *Gammer Gurton's Needle* and *Ralph Roister Doister*, should be read.

2. *Shakespeare*

All Shakespeare's plays should be read and re-read. Useful 'plain text' one-volume editions are published by Oxford University Press and by Blackwells; there are a great many annotated editions of different emphasis and value. For the serious student the 'Arden' edition with one play to a volume is probably the best, but it is costly. The Penguin Shakespeare is useful where cheap copies are wanted for play-readings, and the small edition produced under the supervision of M. R. Ridley is also suitable for pocket or handbag; this gives special attention to textual problems. The Cambridge University Press edition by J. Dover Wilson is also useful. Most editions of Shakespeare brought out by a reputable publisher are of value; but the reader who cares for accuracy, dignity and completeness should avoid the illustrated family volume.

3. *The Other Elizabethans and Jacobeans*

Dramatists who should be read, at least in selections, include: Ben Jonson, Christopher Marlowe, John Ford, Philip Massinger, 'Beaumont and Fletcher', John Webster, Cyril Tourneur, Thomas Middleton, Thomas Dekker, George Chapman.

Suggestions for Further Reading

4. Seventeenth Century

The Puritans closed the theatres for a time, but the student should not forget to read Milton's *Comus* and *Samson Agonistes*, paradoxically, great dramas by a great Puritan. But Milton as a Puritan was himself a paradox.

The Restoration comedies most worth reading today are probably Congreve's *The Way of the World* and *Love for Love*, Wycherley's *The Country Wife* and Dryden's *Marriage à la Mode*.

The heroic drama and rather unsatisfying tragedy of this period would be adequately represented for most students by Dryden's *Don Sebastian* and his best tragedy, *All for Love*.

5. Eighteenth Century

For the average student this period is represented adequately by the plays of Goldsmith and Sheridan, with perhaps a farce by Garrick, or perhaps Garrick and Colman's *The Clandestine Marriage*. It is often possible to pick up minor plays of this period very cheaply indeed in secondhand bookshops.

6. Nineteenth Century

The plays of Byron, Shelley, Keats, Browning and Tennyson are worth reading as poetry, but they are not good stage plays nor representative of the theatre of the time. The student should also try to read a sample play by each of Pinero, Henry Arthur Jones, T. W. Robertson, H. Granville-Barker, perhaps Stephen Phillips, with all Oscar Wilde's plays.

7. Twentieth Century

It is impossible to give suggestions for the study of the twentieth-century drama to see it in perspective, for we are too near to it to be reliable in our judgment. My own suggestions would be: all of Shaw, at least once; his best plays are worth close study; some of Ibsen, because his influence on

203

Suggestions for Further Reading

twentieth-century drama has been great—and at least something by Galsworthy, John Drinkwater, J. M. Barrie, J. B. Priestley, Noel Coward, Terence Rattigan and James Bridie. In the poetic and experimental drama some of the most interesting figures are T. S. Eliot, Christopher Fry, Auden and Isherwood, Louis MacNeice and Anne Ridler. The Irish drama has had a period of great vitality and the student should read some of the plays of J. M. Synge, Sean O'Casey, W. B. Yeats and Lady Gregory.

The acquisition of recent books is always an expensive business. The selection of modern plays available in a county branch library ranges from the remarkable to the deplorable, but librarians are generally very helpful to the student who can ask for something definite. The most recent plays are not usually published until some time after the first production.

8. *Foreign Drama*

Students who can read languages other than English will find a study of other dramas very interesting and much foreign drama, ranging from Molière to Brecht, Japanese dance drama to Strindberg, may be sampled in translation. *The Oxford Companion to the Theatre* should be consulted for details of the drama of other countries.

The American drama presents no great linguistic problem to the British student, who should try to read something by Maxwell Anderson, Arthur Miller, Clifford Odets, Eugene O'Neill, R. E. Sherwood, Thornton Wilder and Tennessee Williams at least.

INDEX

205

Index

206

Index

207

Index

Index

209

Index

Index

211

Index

212